SELF-PORTRAIT
WITH TURTLES

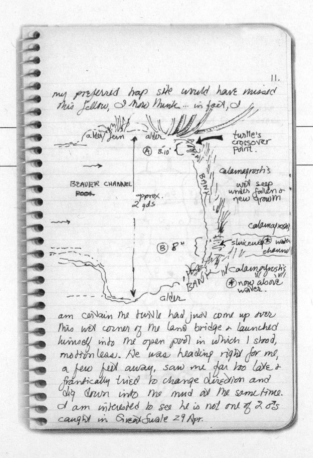

Self-Portrait with Turtles

A Memoir

David M. Carroll

A MARINER BOOK

Houghton Mifflin Company
Boston   New York

David M. Carroll

FIRST MARINER BOOKS EDITION 2005

Visit our Web site: www.houghtonmifflinbooks.com.

Library of Congress Cataloging-in-Publication Data

Carroll, David M.
Self-portrait with turtles : a memoir / David M. Carroll.
p.   cm.
ISBN 0-618-16225-9
1. Turtles.   2. Carroll, David M.   I. Title.

QL666.c5c369 2003
597.92 — dc21   2003047895
ISBN 0-618-16225-9
ISBN 0-618-56584-1 (pbk.)

Book design by Anne Chalmers
Typefaces: Miller, Clarendon

Printed in the United States of America

MP 10 9 8 7 6 5 4 3 2 1

Facing title page: A page from a swamp notebook.

FOR LAURETTE

Acknowledgments

I am much indebted to Harry Foster for suggesting that I write a "more personal" book. Telling him that Memory Lane was not my favorite street, I resisted the idea for some time, but his persistence and persuasion overcame my reluctance. I value the guidance his thorough and thoughtful editing provided in the development of the book. Peg Anderson's dedicated manuscript editing served me well in arriving at the final form, Martha Kennedy's cover design is an absolute gem, and Anne Chalmers's book design superb.

My most supportive agent, Meredith Bernstein, was very influential in my finally deciding to write a memoir centered on my lifelong (since age eight, anyway) connection with turtles. Her enthusiastic reaction to initial drafts of the early years section spurred me on. My wife, Laurette, and daughter Rebecca proved to be invaluable in-house editors for yet another book. They and daughter Riana were critical touchstones throughout this project. Lenita Bofinger's comments on drafts of the early portions of the manuscript were a help and an inspiration, and Joan Beauchemin's readings and responses were a source of great encouragement.

As I wrestled aloud with myself in trying to decide whether to go in the direction of this book, I had many patient ears to hear me and benefited from the insightful comments of listener-friends. Many thanks to Bill Miller, Pamela Getz, Tim Dansdill, Margaret Liszka, Chris Tremblay, June Lisk, Brett Stearns, Greg Van Buiten, Joan Warren, Sally Metheany, Marie Pacetta, Jane Pinel, Pam August, Beulah Bean, and Bill Douglas. And, as with all my books, special thanks to Brian Butler and Ann Campbell Burke.

My greatest debt, of course, is to the turtles.

Contents

EARLY YEARS

What mean these turtles, these coins of the muddy mint issued in early spring? . . . I have seen the signs of spring. I have seen a frog swiftly sinking in a pool, or where he dimpled the surface as he leapt in. I have seen the brilliant spotted tortoises stirring at the bottom of ditches. I have seen the clear sap trickling from the red maples.

—Henry David Thoreau, *Journal*, February 23, 1857

The First Eight Years

CONSECRATED to the God of my parents before my eyes were open, I lived my first eight years in a closed circle of family, relatives, church, and school. I lived in a totally human environment filled with human concerns and considerations. It was a world built by people for people. To the four directions, all horizons were human horizons. All constructs I knew were human constructs, from God on high to carpets and sidewalks underfoot. The physical, intellectual, and emotional aspects of my life had their dawning in a place where there seemed no purpose beyond the getting of the daily bread.

In season I went out to play, but my life was essentially an indoor life. Curtained rooms, a velvety quiet; white lace on the credenza, carefully dusted knickknacks, glass doors closeting cups and saucers, parlor for Sundays. There were stairways and wallpaper, brooding harpy aunts and furtive alcoholic uncles, the clock and the evening paper. There were supper and love and, at times, exceptional wit for relief. My earliest field work lay in reading the faces around me, interpreting gestures, listening to intonations, analyzing turns of phrase. From behind, from a certain angle (I would position myself or wait for him to turn), I could read my father's cheekbones and tell if he'd been drinking. I had to have an idea of how things were going to go.

The difference between inside and outside was not profound. Beyond the door, the steps of furnitured porches descended to sidewalks. Narrow alleys between close, high houses, creepings of moss in crevices of stone or cement where the sun never reached. Backyards, fences, hedgerows of phlox, sweet peas climbing the backs of houses, some butterflies and occasional birds. Sun-blinding summer streets, tightly clipped hedges with spiders and ants; rows of houses ascending hills, homes facing each other in long columns. Porches with gliders, shades lowered against the sun, raised with its passing; people sitting, at almost any hour, overlooking the street. On my walks I crossed the street time and again, seeking passage by vacant porches.

The central Pennsylvania summers were marked by heat and drought. Hot pavement, attic bedrooms hot even in the dead of night; after dark heat lightning always flickered, almost never bringing rain. When afternoon thunderstorms did come, they were torrential. Street floods surged against curbs. Quickly into swimsuits, we kids lay and splashed in gulleys, pavement-heated stormwater's ephemeral streams. There was no detaining this water. Streets and sidewalks steamed and dried in less than a quarter of an hour.

Not far beyond my home and my street were my church and school. Church and school were one, and I in uniform. High stone steeples, dizzyingly high. Cold imposing stone ornamented with stained glass and reaching to heaven. No sun inside; the light of God was a mixture of wavering candlelight and unreachable jeweled gleamings of glass; light enough for crucifixes and tortured saints with strangely serene faces, and for the faithful gathered to pray to them. The purpled, incensed hush sustained a bewildering blend of ecstasy and guilt that I seemed to have no choice but to embrace. Everything in my nature resisted this.

Any corner I turned led to another street. Beyond that lay another street, always lined with houses of other people, and seldom far away, temples to other manifestations of God. For my first eight years I was in a cocoon, awaiting that first swamp, that first turtle.

The First Turtle

At age eight, on June tenth, after supper, on my third day in a new town eight hundred miles from the circumscribed streets I had known all my life, I set out on a walk alone. My new street was called an avenue, and its houses were low units arranged in clusters, imaginatively termed courtyards, in a housing project. Here, in one direction at least, there were not other streets and rows of houses encircling my backyard. To the east, beyond a chain-link fence, parking lot, and ball field, I could see a horizon of trees. I headed there along the fence, passing the back ends of six courtyards. Even the people in my own court were still strangers to me.

I turned a corner and followed the fence to where it ended at the deserted ball field. The woods to the left grew deeper and darker. Windows and rooflines fell away. I could hear no voices. Although I had never been in the woods with anyone, let alone by myself, I did not feel intimidated, but beckoned. Still, I kept to the lighted outer edge of the trees as they dropped to lower, wetter ground. Here I slipped through a dense screen of brush and grassy growth and emerged on the bank of a brook that sparkled out of a darkening swamp. Here was the first border I had ever crossed that did not have the same thing on the other side. The water's slight murmurs and movements among stones and plants were entrancing, and beckoned me even more than the woods.

Frog calls and the sound of intermittent splashings drew me to cross the brook on stepping stones that seemed to have been set out for my passage. A short push through tall, thick growth brought me to an opening at the edge of a pool, where the lowering sun cast an otherworldly light across dark water. It glimmered in dragonfly wings and sporadic silver-beaded sprays tossed up by leaping frogs. Sweet songs from unseen birds drifted on the still air. Everything here was new to me, every sight, sound, and smell a new experience. I doubt my eyes had ever opened wider or tried harder to take in my surroundings. I was in another world, a new world utterly distinct from any I had known. It was all the more miraculous for being real.

For some time I stood still, absorbing, becoming absorbed. A shivering intensity came over me, all my senses became heightened; it was as though I had new senses. Stirrings in the reeds caught my eye. Not far from my watching-place, with slow deliberate movements that caused partings and closings in a bed of emergent grassy growth, something moved in the water. After a long pause, more stirrings. I had no picture to go by, no idea what to expect, as I waited for something to become visible. More jostlings. Afraid to move, lest I frighten away whatever was on the prowl, I continued to wait and watch. Even before I saw my first turtle, in watching and attempting to interpret these reedy shiftings, I began to develop one of the search-images that was to become a foundation of the rest of my life.

At length a small section of the outer fringe of reeds was pushed aside and a turtle appeared in the shallows, moving slowly, gracefully over the bottom, so at ease, at home underwater. I was transfixed. How could any living thing be marked like this? The turtle was as black as jet and adorned with radiant yellow and orange; head, legs, and tail aglow with scatterings of spots, intense blazings of orange at the sides of her head, markings all the more brilliant for being seen through clear water. I was spellbound by her patterns and the way she moved. With the living vision of this turtle at its center, the realm I had entered came all the more to life for me. Everything I was seeing and feeling suddenly became magnified. I was keenly fascinated by the frogs and dragonflies and all, but this turtle . . . Her cautious black head turned slowly left and right. I could see her pale orange face, her black and amber-gold eyes.

Shaking all over, barely breathing, I watched her. I had to hold that turtle but was frozen by the feelings surging through me. Shifting her eyes toward the surface, the turtle saw me. She began to turn back into the reeds. I was afraid that I might never see her again. I could not let her get away. Suddenly I was in the water, shoes and all, my hand closing over the jeweled dome of her carapace.

A spotted turtle hiding in sedge for the night.

Back up on the banking, I marveled at the feel of the turtle in my trembling hands. It was as if I had been allowed to clasp life itself in my hands. How could I begin to imagine all that was represented by a connection this tangible; the smooth, flat bottom shell resting on my left palm, the caressable contour of the perfect dome of her top shell lying beneath the fingertips of my right hand. Gradually, with great caution, the turtle came forth from her shell. I could see no more than the tip of her nose for some minutes, then her spectacular head (so close now) and gracefully extending neck. The deep eyes of the wild living thing I held in my hands appeared so calm. Holding that first turtle and looking into her eyes, I bonded inextricably with her kind and her world. She became the center of an endlessly expanding universe within the universe.

Her wild eyes imparted patience. But her legs began to reach out of the protection of her shell, tentatively at first, then suddenly with resistance, struggling against my hands with spasmodic thrusts.

I couldn't let her go. I carried her home with me. I was only beginning to sort out, to learn. It would take a regrettably long time for me to understand that no turtle should be taken from its place.

With that first turtle I crossed a boundary of greater dimensions than I can ever fully comprehend. I changed lives within a life, worlds within a world. Metamorphosis . . . I had wings now, and different eyes; the sun was not the same. I could not yet name a plant or animal around me, except in the most general terms: "grass," "bird," "frog," "turtle." I had no idea what kind of turtle I had found, and when I asked someone in my neighborhood the next day, I was told that it was a "sun turtle." It was certainly a turtle of the sun to me.

Turtle was the alphabet of a new language, and not only a passkey into a new world but a key to open the gate of a world I knew I had to leave. The entering was immediate, the opening I saw before me extended forever. I never turned back, though the leaving was gradual, much of it a struggle. The swamp, the marsh, looking for turtles, being there; every time I went out was a reaffirmation. It was too real for superstition and far exceeded magic. I needed no ritual, no priest or priestess, shaman, intercessor, or interpreter. I needed only my eyes, ears, hands and feet, awakening mind, and deepening intuition. I didn't even need a map. I was home.

The morning after I found the first turtle I was out again, back again; passing along the fence, turning the corner, leaving houses and yards behind with an almost unbearable eagerness. With gathering elation I slipped among the alders. It had not been a dream. The screen awaited, and on the other side of it the brook still sparkled on. The stepping stones awaited me; the sweet rank growth of summer along the stream was all the more fragrant in the morning. I watched the water sliding by. Where to go? What watery route to follow? I had never entered the heart of a day before. This was not just an evening run; the landscape and the whole day spread out before me, and hidden somewhere within them, there had to be another turtle. Here was a returning I could almost taste. From the first entering I knew I would have to come back at every chance.

I crossed the brook on stones I would walk countless times over the next ten years and retraced the route that had led me to the first turtle. A lifelong quest whose dimensions I could not begin to grasp, had no need to grasp, had begun on a single turning in time. Spotted turtle was touchstone and magnet. In searching for the turtle, following the turtle, I was drawn into the turtle's world. I discovered what seemed to me a limitless landscape, with the turtle at its center. I had crossed to Turtle Island.

The spotted turtle's world was different from mine, yet it was a world I could enter, and come to be in. It was unknown but not alien, a world of endless revelation and abiding mystery. From my first solitary setting-out as an eight-year-old boy I was never afraid. Though uneasy at times, on the rare occasions when I became lost for a while, I was never afraid. I was where I belonged. I began to map the world I had entered by mapping the turtle's world. In a pattern that would persist throughout my life, water led me on to more turtles, turtles led me on to new waters. And so my landscape, laced with waterways, unfolded.

There were pressures, spoken and unspoken, that would keep me at home, have me stay in my neighborhood . . . chores to do . . .

wasn't my house good enough? To go off to the swamps and woods was to abandon—in some measure to reject—home, family, and community. Human social units have a tendency to feel threatened by one who moves apart, particularly by one who goes toward the nonhuman. In the face of many uncertainties people seek reassurance, the reinforcement that they find in having a family stick close together, always having others be near them, never out of contact— thinking like them, saluting the same flag, attending the same church. A psychological and spiritual, even a physical, confinement becomes established, a subtle, binding entrapment. One who strays afield can come to feel the communal critique for separating out and be in for a difficult time.

I relished the days when I could feel free to walk out the door and leave the yard, to go back out to my new world and take the turtle day as my own. I meant no slight in setting out and could never understand why this could not be more freely given. But I could not wait for it to be granted. I knew that I had to take it for myself, no matter the risk, the eventual cost. At times I had to slip away, go out into the heart of that great glad day, not thinking ahead, letting what would come at the end of the day come. From the finding of the first turtle I became a time bandit, watching faces and the clock, the corner of my eye ever on the door.

Compañera

I was alone when I found the first spotted turtle, and over the years I would need to be alone to achieve my greatest awareness of the turtles and their places and find my deepest sense of being there. But in third grade, as my first full turtle season was beginning, I found one whom I wanted to bring into my outdoor world. She bonded with it at once. Although not always together, we were inseparable, and bound to swamp and stream, field and wood.

She could run faster than most boys, and certainly faster than I.

Even in boyhood I walked far more often than I ran. "You have two speeds, David," my father told me. "Slow and all stop." I jogged when the goal was to get to a certain place, but once I entered the wilds, I mostly walked. Like a turtle, I had endurance, not speed. I walked and waded all day long. And always slowly, for the moment I slipped through one of those screens of brush I was where I wanted to be, and the more slowly I moved, the longer I kept still, the more I would see. My swift companion had that patience, too; her dark eyes searched with a similar focus. We would separate, fanning out to different shallows in a pool or working the opposite banks of a stream, calling out to each other when there was something that had to be looked at.

We parted grasses and sedges, peered into the water, stirred mud and leaves, searched under rocks and logs. We looked at whatever we could not catch and shared brief holdings of anything we could get our hands on. From the beginning I had a way of pulling turtles out of nowhere. Once, at the edge of a small pond on her grandmother's property, among tree roots at an undercut bank, I saw a bit of a pattern of yellow spots in black water. I called out to her, and as she came near I reached in and caught the turtle. When I pulled my capture up to show her, I found that I had two turtles in hand. The dark-faced male whose shell I gripped was clasping an orange-faced female. Despite the dramatic intrusion, he would not let go of her. I set them back in place at once.

She lived in a cottage on her grandmother's lingering estate, in circumstances at least as economically stringent as mine, perhaps more stringent. She was the only girl, with five or six brothers. I never really knew her family. Our shared world existed away from both of our houses. Sometimes, though, especially if rain came on, we'd visit her grandmother. Her grandfather had died some time before. He had been in the China trade, and there were marvelous paintings, sculptures, furnishings, and carpets in every room. I always spent some time looking at a large Chinese screen painting, ink on silk, a landscape with high mountain peaks, twisted pines, clouds, and flying cranes. On some occasions her grandmother read stories to us from Ernest Thompson Seton's *Wild Animals I Have Known.*

We were rather like wild animals ourselves, always quick to be out of doors, rarely even meeting indoors, but by some pond or stream. Off in the woods, following brooks, we made altars of moss and leaves, branches, stones, and wildflowers. We dug claylike silt from a spotted-turtle stream near my house and made pottery vessels, leaving them to dry on stones. We made sailboats from autumn leaves and set them adrift in breezes over the spotted-turtle pond by her house.

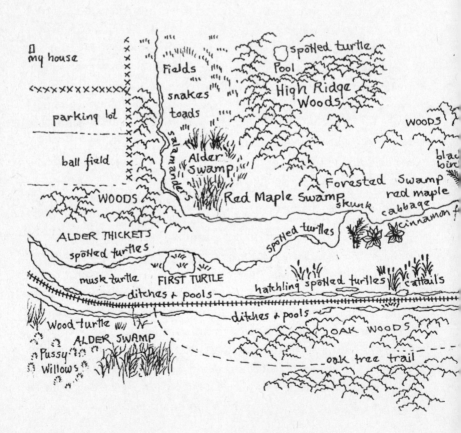

Her pond drained into a salt marsh via a narrow stream that glimmered between mossy banks, fresh water's final run before entering the sound. We caught elvers in this brooklet, tiny eels impossibly journeyed from the Sargasso Sea and were en route to their six-to eight-year life in fresh water before returning to the great salt sea. We walked the salt marsh along tidal creeks alive with fiddler crabs. At times we rowed over the tidal flats and caught blueshell crabs. At low tide we could wade a shoal to a little island ringed with seaweed-covered rocks and forested with oak. A stranded brass-studded chest always portended treasure, but every time we opened it, the trunk held no more than the nest of a field mouse.

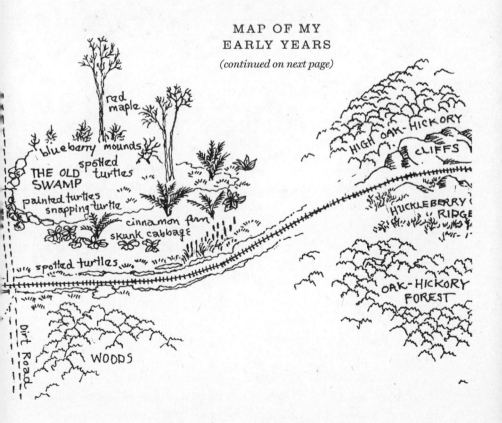

MAP OF MY
EARLY YEARS

(continued on next page)

red maple

blueberry mounds

THE OLD SWAMP

spotted turtles

painted turtles

snapping turtle

cinnamon fern

skunk cabbage

spotted turtles

Dirt Road

WOODS

HIGH OAK-HICKORY

CLIFFS

HUCKLEBERRY RIDGE

OAK-HICKORY FOREST

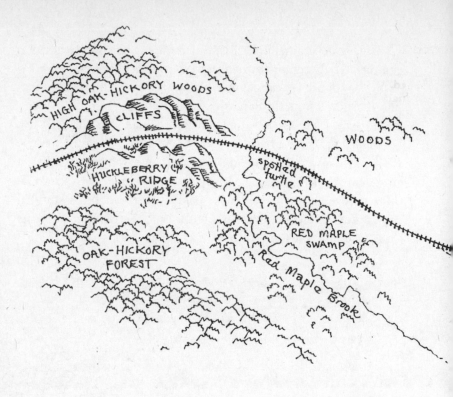

One summer she gave me a present: *Reptiles and Amphibians,* a Golden Nature Guide, with page after page of full-color illustrations of turtles, snakes, lizards, frogs, toads, salamanders, and newts. The accounts of their life histories were fascinating, although I supposed I never would go where most of them lived, and so had no expectation of seeing them in the wild. But some of the local ones I already knew well, and others I would try to find. The pages featuring those that I had spent so much time among electrified me—time and again I turned to page 40, with its spotted turtle. Here was a part of myself, part of what I lived for, pictured and storied in a book.

I wanted to give my friend a gift for her eleventh birthday. Searching in a watery ditch that ran along the railroad tracks, I discovered, among obscuring shadows in a small opening in mats of

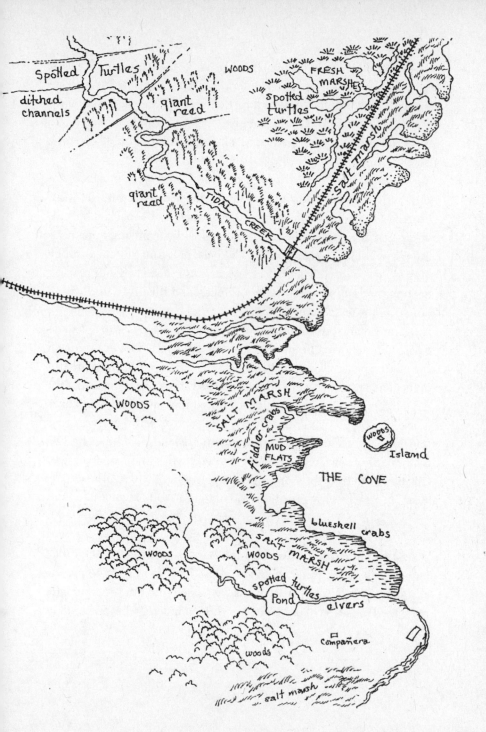

fallen cattail, a single yellow spot, signaling the carapace of a baby spotted turtle. My eyes were keen, my search-images becoming ever sharper. I was not looking for a turtle for her, I was just looking for turtles, as I always did. I did not give turtles to people. But as I held this exquisite little one, I saw it as a living jewel she could keep for a time.

While turtles slept through the winter, we were in school together. It was not the same as our wild-hearted hours in wild-hearted places. The end of our outdoor season was marked by end-of-day partings as darkness overtook us with surprising quickness, the air chilling down suddenly. The base of a railroad cut through high stone ledge, cliffs halfway between our houses, was our place of parting. A clasping and kissing of hands and turning away toward home, a mile or so for each of us.

She would start off on a run. I jogged, then slowed to a walk as I passed the red-maple swamp where some spotted turtles went for the winter, part of what I called the Old Swamp. I took deep breaths of its dank autumn scent and scanned its bits of silver, the last of the day's light on its silent water, a sky-tinted mirror leaded with sharp black lines of red maple and alder. I had come to know its every rock and log, every blueberry and red maple island, to know the Old Swamp in somewhat the way its spotted turtles knew it. Once past this place (no time for stopping in) I picked up my pace, the stream along the tracks providing a thread of light to follow.

It seemed there would always be another day. But in seventh grade I entered the public junior high school and she went away to private school. I did not follow her, and as we passed into our separate later lives, the landscape of our time together completely disappeared.

Another Spring

Weakened by thaw, the outer edge of a great ice sheet gradually gives way under my weight and eases me into two and a half feet of mud and water, floodwater filled with the new light of spring. On the twenty-second of March I begin the first day of my fiftieth year with the turtles. In a far different place I set out on the same search, with the intent and eagerness and much of the heart, if not the legs, of the original, even aboriginal, boy. My eyes are not as keen as they were; I now see more by way of experience and a long accrual and sharpening of search-images. As I peer into water pockets blacker than shadow and scan sedges burnished by winter and reflecting the near-blinding ascendant March sun, I am grateful that I still have a turtle place to come to and that I can find a way to be here.

So much opens up before me at this annual returning. The midday quiet here—not even a whisper from the water gliding by—the stillness and apparent torpor of the snowy woods and ice-bound alder thickets I crossed in coming here belie the urgency of turtle season about to break. The need to be everywhere at once is never greater than during the first few days of the turtles' emergence from hibernation: there are so many beginnings, renewals, and first instants set in such simultaneity. Every place I am is a hundred I am not. I never have a harder time reining myself in, focusing, slowing into the day. There is such a rush within the tranquility and timelessness of thaw, the stunned, blinking coming forth in so many hidden places, all in the space of any hour, any moment; somewhere, everything.

I have been watching turtles in this great wetland mosaic for twenty-seven years; fifteen years ago a turtle led me to discover this corner within it, one of the most significant habitats of my turtle life, a place of water and sedge, shrub and fern mounds, spotted turtles, knowledge, and mystery. In my mind it is linked with seasons past, with turtles and turtle places that no longer exist. Memory and renewal . . . I come back for another season. Who is still here? Who is no longer here? Who is here that I have yet to know, will never come to know?

I look for many, but one in particular has become the touchstone of each year's searching, a spotted turtle I have followed, as best I can follow a turtle, for at least eighteen years. During my first years of coming here, after fleeing from a place where the wetlands had become unbearably diminished, I went out to be there, to observe, to become lost and found in what surrounded me, as I had done as a boy. I was naturalist as artist-poet, not yet having added the dimension of field biologist. This turtle was among the first I began to track in a new way.

At my presentations on turtles and wetlands, I am often asked, especially in elementary schools, "Do you have names for your turtles?"

"No," I always respond initially, "I don't think of them as 'my' turtles, or as pets or as people with shells. They are wild animals with a unique history on earth that dates back more than two hundred and fifty million years." Then I pause. "But I must confess that I do have names for several spotted turtles I have known in the wild for a long time." And I go on to tell them about Ariadne. When I first found her, she struck me as a particularly beautiful turtle, and I decided that rather than listing her as "female spotted turtle number 57," I would give her a beautiful name in my notebooks. Ariadne has provided me key insights into the life history of her kind and has become emblematic of every spotted turtle I have seen. For many springs now, a central theme of my searches for the first turtles up from hibernation has been "looking for Ariadne."

As I search for her in this shrub swamp today, I also have an eye out for another turtle, the one who led me to discover this overwintering sanctuary. For several years I had wondered where the spotted turtles I found in vernal pools and backwater fens went for the winter. Seeking them in shallow still-water red-maple swamps and sedgy marshes, the kinds of habitats in which I had seen them emerge from hibernation in milder coastal areas to the south, I was looking in the wrong places. Thinking that some deeper pocket in this great shrub swamp might serve as a hibernaculum, I made a dedicated mound-by-mound search here. Well into the afternoon I spotted two vertebral scutes of a turtle's carapace, dry, with a dull, shadowy luster and subdued spots, showing through the fern duff and dried-leaf covering of a hidden basking place on a mound of red maple and royal fern. The sighting gave me as much of a start as had that of the first spotted turtle. The instant I saw her, I knew I had found one of the niches where the spotted turtles wintered. Like Ariadne, this turtle was an adult female with a well-worn shell. This discovery occurred on the thirteenth of April; I decided to name a second turtle, and entered her in my notebook as "13 April."

In its seemingly magical way, the water in this compartment of the floodplain wetland has warmed to 42 degrees, even though it is ringed with ice shelves, and the neighboring still-water wetlands, where painted turtles hibernate, are frozen over. The heavy shrub and sedge growth here acts as a solar collector, radiating heat that melts the ice, and the steady drift of floodwater from the permanent stream 250 yards away further erodes the frozen mantle. This seasonal hydrology, along with the mucky substrate and exceedingly dense underwater weavings of roots and rhizomes in shrub, sedge, and fern mounds, accounts for the spotted turtles' coming here to avoid freezing and escape detection by predators over the winter. These characteristics serve as my revised model as I search for new places where spotted turtles might hibernate. In some of these habitats they are joined on occasion by snapping turtles, and some winters by young Blanding's turtles.

A deep and abiding uneasiness tempers the elation I once felt during my first wadings of the year. My long history with turtles has been marked time and again by loss of place, by the physical and spiritual annihilation of the landscape, compelling me to move on in search of wilder places. Over the past decade I have witnessed an inexorable encroachment on this landscape and its ecology. Every spring now I wonder how much longer I will be able to come here and where I can turn next.

Red-winged blackbirds call, gently drifting water glimmers by, heat waves dance from dry, sun-flooded sedge. Slowly retracing familiar channels, I wade into the birth of another spring. Wind out of the southeast soughs in the pines of the bordering upland rise, fairly roars through them at times, but in this low-lying wetland it barely stirs the sedges. At 2:32 in the afternoon I catch sight of the first turtle of my fiftieth turtle-following year. A young one, she appears stunned by the brilliance of these first hours out of hibernation, the cold of the past winter still lingering in her. I pick her up and see two notches on the marginal plates of her carapace, marks I make in recording individual turtles. I can't remember when I first encountered her, but the date is in one of my past notebooks. The annuli on her plastron show that she is twelve years old. If she survives for another eight years she will become a breeding adult. If she lives as long as Ariadne, she will probably outlive me. And if her habitat stays as it is, she is likely to live decades beyond her threshold breeding age.

My concern deepens as I wade on. I feel uneasy that I haven't seen more than one turtle by now. There is an apprehensiveness in my first searches of the year that I can't shake until I begin to see numbers of turtles. The habitats themselves are my first concern: Have the upland margins been cleared for development? Have drainage ditches been dug, culverts put in, beaver dams torn out? I know others who study turtles who have had the populations they follow decimated by collectors. In this area, however, human disruptions have not occurred as far as I can tell. I begin to think that natural causes might account for the fact that I have found only one turtle. We have had a record three hundred days without snow, extending back into the previous winter. Without an insulating snow cover, this wetland might have frozen so deeply that turtles froze to death. Or predators such as otters could have gotten them. Or perhaps a change in hydrology or water chemistry or a transition in the plant composition caused the turtles to shift their overwintering grounds. For all that I have come to know of these turtles from my long association with them and from other field workers and scientists, I begin each season wondering if I really know anything at all.

At 3:40 P.M. I find a second spotted turtle, another subadult perhaps only minutes up from her fourteenth hibernation. Eyes closed, she rests on a mound formed by sweet gale, alder, and royal fern. Stems of meadowsweet and steeplebush, some broken by winter's winds and the weight of ice, help to conceal her. She too has notches on her carapace, meaning I have recorded her in past notebooks. From what I know of this place and the turtles' seasonal timings, I feel I should have seen four to six of them by now. "It is early, it is still so early," I keep telling myself.

The sun hangs low over the distant western hills. Out along the margins of the permanent stream whose floodwaters sustain this winter stronghold, red-winged blackbirds take up the communal calling that marks afternoon's transition to evening from the time of the first openings in the ice until summer. I wade out of the densest zone of shrubs and ferns to a more open sedge meadow. At a narrow turning I am jolted by the startling black and orange markings of a spotted turtle's plastron; I never see a living turtle on its back.

When my son was very young, he asked as he held a wood turtle, "Does it hurt turtles to be on their backs?"

"It isn't good for them—they can't breathe properly," I answered.

"Then why do they make them so beautiful on the bottom?" he asked.

I wade to the plastron that glows softly in shallow water. On a sunken mat of sedge, the empty shell lies upside down. I retrieve it from the water and turn it over. On the tooth-scraped carapace there are notches on the twelfth left and eighth right marginals: male number fifteen. His low, broad shell and distinctive decorations are very familiar to me; I knew him for more than a decade. He was a brightly marked, prominent member of this colony, active in this wetland and the large, grassy vernal pool to which many of the turtles who overwinter here migrate for the peak of their feeding and breeding season. Except for some skin remaining between his carapace and plastron at front and back, his shell has been cleaned out—head, limbs, tail, interior bones all gone. The vibrant, living yellow of his markings has faded to pale bone white. He was probably taken by a predator last fall, perhaps during a final mate-seeking excursion before he went into hibernation.

All that remains of the turtle's life is this final architectural structure, an enduring representation of the unique adaptation of the rib cage to enclose the shoulder and pelvic girdles and even allow the head to be withdrawn inside it. This skeletal arrangement, which distinguishes turtles from all other vertebrate groups that have appeared on earth, fits into my palm just as the shell of the first living turtle I held did. I close my eyes. The form of the shell describes the life it held for so long. How many times did I hold this shell while it held that life? Turtle shell becomes memory stone.

I run my fingers over his shell and look into the space between carapace and plastron, imagining the life this bony fortress encased until its defense was at last to no avail. This shell first appeared aboveground when, as a hatchling, the turtle dug out of a nest after an incubation of one hundred days or so. He at once took up his nest-to-water journey, his orientation to the wetland habitat required by his species. He may have spent his first winter within twenty yards of where his shell lies now, emerging from nearly half a year insensate to take up basking and finally feeding for the first time, at the outset of his first growing season, some ten months after his mother secreted in the earth the egg that cradled him. For ten years or so he probably kept close to the marsh-bordered shrub-swamp compartment where he first wintered. In his second decade he began to wander, mapping the world of his kind in the broader landscape, until around age twenty he took his place as one of the colony's breeding adults. It was in this phase of his life that I first found him.

He survived against the great odds and intense selective pressure that hatchling spotted turtles face in reaching adulthood, which takes twenty years or so in this part of his species' range. He had not yet taken on the appearance of an older turtle and it seems reasonable to think he could have lived for decades more. I wonder how it goes with these turtles, how for so many years they live unscathed among the agents that can, on the turning of a single moment, bring an end to that life, and the potential for longevity that is so unusual among wild animals. Tooth marks have cut through the black lamina of his carapace and left scorings and broader scrapes that reveal the white bone beneath. The teeth that inflicted these wounds were small, almost needlelike. His shell, beautiful even though its once-brilliant spots have faded in death, is not cracked or broken. I have seen far more severe gougings and chewings, inflicted by bigger teeth and stronger jaws, on the shells of living turtles. I cannot guess what predator overtook him in an unguarded moment, caught him too far from escape cover, and managed to overpower his court of last resort, his withdrawal into his shell. Probably it was a variety of scavengers that cleaned out his shell so thoroughly.

Only rarely do I learn the fates of the turtles I follow. For most there is only one last record in a notebook, and beyond that I don't know whether the turtle has died, been taken into captivity, simply eluded me, or migrated beyond the rounds I make. My last note does not necessarily imply the end of a life, and many I have recorded will outlive me.

Leaving the water and climbing back up on the ice shelf, I nearly pass by a spotted turtle in tussock sedge on an alder mound, but my eyes sweep back to register her presence in a shadowy chamber arched by a swirled confusion of sedge. Nearly all of my turtle sightings begin with a detail detected by peripheral vision. Extremely well concealed, she basks as a shadow among shadows, barely revealed by a shaft of sunlight. The concern that has mounted in me over the course of the day is eased by this sighting of an adult who has safely emerged from winter's lengthy grip. She does not move. Like a wood turtle, she relies on a camouflaging blend of light and shade and mazes of vegetation to keep her from being detected;

13 April, basking cryptically.

she will not risk movement that would reveal her in a situation where it would be difficult to elude a predator. When I pick her up, I immediately recognize the shape and markings of 13 April, who provided the initial clue to this place fifteen years ago, basking then even more cryptically about fifty yards from where she hides and warms herself today. Among the turtles I have come to know here, she has struck me as being exceptionally dedicated to hiding, even when she is not sunning herself; I rarely encounter her during the active season. Is this an individual characteristic, possibly a trait she passes on to her progeny and thereby contributes to her species?

Here is another spotted turtle's chapter, this not a final one, at the dawning of another spring.

Wild Boy

During my first full summer in the swamps, after finding more spotted turtles in the backwater pooling where I had seen the first, I began to roam farther. Every fifty or a hundred yards was a new territory. I passed through a narrow wood and came to a railroad track with watery ditches along both sides of its raised bed, slow and shallow streamings with pockets and pools, luxurious with marshy growth, low grassy sweeps, and intermittent cattail stands. Spotted turtles lived here too.

I ranged along the railroad bed, which was bounded by woods: high, dry oak forest on one side and low, wet red-maple swamp on the other. Once or twice a day slow-moving trains came by. Otherwise I was as good as alone in a wilderness. I crept through tall ferns and braved head-high blackberry canes, looking into the water, and waded the ditches barefoot. Up the tracks I came to an old dirt road and followed it, discovering a large, open, weedy pond ringed with velvet-mossed islands crowned with blueberry shrubs and red maples. It was alive with the twanging of green frogs, the resonant thrumming of bullfrogs, glitterings of insect wings, and calling of blackbirds. This wooded swamp was the Okefenokee in comparison with my first turtle pool. If I could so easily find so much in that first little backwater, what would I find here?

The promise that hung so heavily in the summer air did not fail me: during my first hour along the swamp's shallow margins I saw the pale orange face of a spotted turtle regarding me from dense mats of grassy growth. I rolled up my pants as high as I could and waded to where I saw her go down, but there was no finding this turtle. Catching one in the Old Swamp, with its broader and deeper waters, mucky bottom, deadfall trees, and Sargasso Sea–like vegetation, would be no easy matter.

Day after day that first summer I traversed the alder thickets, the red-maple woods with its skunk-cabbage-and-fern-bordered brook and spotted-turtle backwaters, the ditches along the train tracks, and especially the Old Swamp. With an eye out for turtles, I kept closely to wet places, but I was also fascinated by toads, salamanders, and snakes, and I took to field and forest to find them at times. Every meadow or wood, and especially any stream or pool, all of these theaters of summer taken together, held no end of spellbinding forms, colors, and patterns, moving in a seasonal rhythm of life habits I was only beginning to decipher. And these places they lived in—places of water, stone, and plants; sunlight and shadow; water lilies, reeds, and ferns; mossy hummocks, grassy swirls, and blackberry tangles; woods and shrub thickets with drifts of leaves;

A turtle basking in a marsh.

grassy fields—all joined to create one great landscape. I entered, came to know, the design of this living landscape before I knew any of the specific definitions of that elusive word "design." And as I moved through it I felt myself part of the pattern, or at the very least a witness to it.

The sheer joy of being there, of simply bearing witness, continued to be paramount. I went out neither to heal my heartbreaks nor to celebrate my happinesses, but to be in nature and outside of myself. Turtles, spotted turtles most significantly, were a living text moving upon an endless turning of the pages of the natural world. I read a natural history that breathed. The moment I went out to meet it, it would open up before me. Each time out I could enter anew. An ongoing learning experience, or experience-learning, it called for a lack of confusion, a focus and dedication I wanted to give.

Once I got away to the swamps the sun seemed to stay in the sky forever. I had no watch and lost track of the time as soon as I left my house. Turtle time was best unmeasured. The end of the day always took me by surprise, and I had to learn to keep an eye on the lengthening shadows of late afternoon, to leave enough time for my shoes and socks to dry. I took them off to go after turtles but invariably managed to get them soaked, and it went much better for me if I got home dry-shod and on time for supper.

※

As summer waned and autumn came on, I felt a sense of loss I had never experienced before. Over the course of my first full season I had become Turtle Boy. When summer vacation ended, that tremendous richness of time, in which hours could pass unnumbered and days go unnamed, was over.

Feeling far removed from turtles as I watched the leaves fall, I found solace in the school library. I had always loved books—their feel and smell, the pleasure of opening a new book and turning its pages, of being read to, reading, and looking at illustrations. My mother had read fairy tales and other stories to my brother and me, and she bought us a set of children's classics as we got older: *Robin Hood, King Arthur and His Knights of the Round Table, The Swiss Family Robinson, The Adventures of Huckleberry Finn, The Jungle Book,* and others. Now I was attracted to books that might not have caught my eye before my summer in the swamps.

I found a beautifully written book about a frog with naturalistic drawings depicting his life and surroundings. Just the existence of such a book gave me the shivers. I was all the more entranced because the story included a turtle, even though he was relegated to a minor and fairly lamebrained role, and the drawing of him was the only one in the book that wasn't naturalistic. Again and again I signed out *Wagtail,* never tiring of reading the tale of the little frog and his compatriots in Blue Pool; though anthropomorphized, the account was true enough to nature that I could equate it with what I saw in real pools, with actual frogs and turtles. I looked long and hard at the illustrations, graphite renderings printed in green ink, which were even more evocative of the world I had bonded so strongly with than the captivating text.

The little library was rich in animal stories, and I went on to read them all, classics such as *Carcajou the Wolverine, The Grizzly King,* and *Tarka the Otter.* I also discovered a remarkable field guide, Ann Haven Morgan's *Field Book of Ponds and Streams,* which described and illustrated the lives I was getting to know. I revered the color plates of salamanders and frogs, and especially plate xxiii, with its "two common pond turtles" in vivid color: the spotted turtle and the painted turtle. The account of wood-turtle mating convinced me that those intriguing stories I was hearing about where babies come from were not without foundation.

Even more astonishing was Holling C. Holling's great saga of a turtle, *Minn of the Mississippi,* the life story of a snapping turtle interwoven with a history of the Mississippi River. The margins of the book's large pages were filled with extraordinary, lifelike drawings of snapping turtles, from hatchlings to full-grown ones. Nature drawings surrounded the text on every page, and full-page watercolors showed the most dramatic scenes from the life of Minn.

I was granted permission to enter the gated special collection at the back of the library in the city next to my town, where I found more books on turtles: Raymond L. Ditmars's *The Reptile Book*, and Clifford H. Pope's *Turtles of the United States and Canada*, as well as the ultimate reference on the subject, the recently published *Handbook of Turtles*, by Archie Carr, which greatly expanded upon Pope's work of 1939. I would check out Pope and Carr for two weeks, return them, wait a week, then go back to take them out again. The next year I asked for Carr's book for Christmas. When my mother saw the price, she was taken aback and said that if I got that gift there wouldn't be anything else. I assured her that if I got that book I wouldn't need another present. All I got for Christmas was Carr's *Handbook of Turtles*.

Despite all these books and my school friends, winter was interminable. When the water chilled down so much that I was unable to find turtles, I looked for snakes after school, making searches in a brushy field. Even after the trees were bare I could find them, curled up beneath boards and stones still warm from the day's sun: baby and adult garter, northern brown, redbelly, and smooth green snakes.

As autumn deepened, I took up a practice that became one of the banes of my mother's existence. I brought in cocoons, leaves, special rocks, clumps of earth, even chunks of frozen turf hacked from streambanks. The latter came to life under the indoor sun of the gooseneck lamp on my desk: sprouts came forth from roots and seeds; tendrils, stems, and shafts emerged from thawing mud. The veneer of my desk buckled and split from constant thaws, seeps, and the occasional inaccurate watering. A praying mantis egg case launched what seemed to be hundreds of perfect, pale, minute replicas of the menacing-looking adults. My desk became an omnium-gatherum of cherished bits of the wild outdoor world I had such a hard time relinquishing to winter. I sprouted a potato in a glass of water. I kept a little spotted turtle and bought two dime-store sliders, but not even these could substitute for the seasons and places I had had to surrender to school and the hard cold.

At the earliest hint of spring, I began walking the brooks and ditches and visiting the Old Swamp. The red-winged blackbirds had come back, but it was still too early for turtles. I had started my life with turtles the previous June, well into their active season, and I didn't know exactly where to look or what to look for when I set out to find them coming out of hibernation. For all the life histories in reference books, there was so much more to be learned from being there, from observing the turtles in their habitats. I didn't find any in my early searches of the brook and its backwater or in the railroad ditches. And on a warm, sunny afternoon in mid-March, as I stole into the blackbird-singing Old Swamp, there was still no sign of a turtle. But, though I had never before witnessed the phenomenon, I sensed an imminent explosion of life. I cautiously circled the swamp's sodden borders, hopping from mossy stone to mossy log or tree root, waiting and watching the water from behind red maples. A dull sheen caught my eye as I scanned shrub-thicketed island mounds, their velvet-mossed carpetings more vibrantly green than ever. On a mound, reflected in the water, a carapace partly screened by a maze of twigs glowed softly in the sun that was bringing its bearer back to life. Then I made out two more turtles, together on an island, and a fourth on a sedge hummock nearby. After the long winter sleep, absolutely motionless and partially hidden, they were giving themselves up to the rays of the sun that would fire the long season before them.

I had found a secret corner of the Old Swamp where some of the turtles went to spend the winter. A dream of spring had become reality. The light on their shells . . . I could hardly take in what I was looking at. I had kept an appointment with the turtles and, through them, with the year itself, an appointment I would devote the rest of my life to keeping. From that moment on, every spring would have the feeling of this first spring. This was my New Year's Day. All at

A spotted turtle in the rain.

once an endless summer opened before me. I was beginning to learn. Other than an almost instinctive, accruing knowledge there was nothing here that could be carried away; images and experiences faded as I left. There was nothing tangible that I could take back with me. Not even the turtles, if I were to take barefoot to ice-water and manage to catch one or two. I did take turtles out at times, too often, but nothing came with them, really. So much is left behind. One can only go back to it. It all moves as life and time move and can only be encountered along the way. The place must be there, the wild and sacred meeting ground. Once it is lost, the bond is broken, and all that was found there disappears.

Over that second turtle summer, the ninth summer of my life, I continued to expand my network of turtle places, moving beyond the Old Swamp. I added painted, snapping, and musk turtles to my repertoire. But my first watery hollows and their brooks remained my center, and there I continued to spend most of my days. I became more familiar with plants, getting to know some well enough to eat them, browsing wintergreen-tasting bark and the buds of black birch twigs in spring, blueberry flowers in May, the berries themselves later on. Blackberries were abundant along the railroad beds, and huckleberries among boulders and ledges on some of the oak ridges. In autumn I dug duck potatoes, the tubers of broad-leaved arrowhead, and boiled them on fires made of dead branches circled with stones.

In shallower waterholds I would slide, alligator-like, into the water and deep muck. Stretched out full length, with only my head above the water, I was far less conspicuous to turtles than when I waded. Occasionally I could slide along and slip close enough to a basking turtle to grab it before it tumbled into the water. I groped about for unseen turtles in murky, algae-filled water, dense mats of submergent vegetation, and mud.

When I set my hand down on a snapping turtle he would sometimes surge away, but more often he'd hold still as I gingerly ran my fingertips over the smooth or mossy carapace, seeking the saw-toothed rear margin by which I could catch him. When I did take hold, he would struggle mightily and with great strength to get away but would begin striking and snapping only if I lifted him out of the water. A snapper never attacked me in the water.

In search of musk turtles, I slid and groped through an even shallower, muckier pond, a warm, green soup of algae. The carapaces of these small, extremely cryptic turtles usually were covered with algae for added camouflage. They rarely put more than their pinpoint nostrils above the surface, and only at intervals of an hour or more. One day while groping for musk turtles, I felt a fiery sting that shot through my hand. All the joints on my right hand began to swell, and gradually my elbow did as well. For three days I couldn't close my hand and could barely bend my elbow. After I was taken to the doctor for shots, the swellings gradually subsided. I suspect that a giant water bug bit me when I inadvertently pinned it down with my hand. Because of this experience, and my increasing tendency to get itchy, swollen reactions to the leeches that became attached to me as I slid through the water, I abandoned this highly successful method of looking for turtles.

Wandering farther along the railroad tracks, I found yet more streams and marshes bordering brackish creeks well beyond the Old Swamp. I walked through forests of giant reeds, and found spotted turtles in long, narrow ditches. Straight as an arrow and no doubt man-made, these channels of fresh water just above the saline margins of lower tidal creeks had probably been dug for drainage in an effort to control mosquitoes. Now they were water-filled and bordered by heavy cover, so spotted turtles had appropriated them.

The trains that passed through were so slow-moving that I would occasionally hop onc and jump off at the Old Swamp or a little farther down the line. From various points along the high railroad embankment I could look down and discover low-lying marshes and streams. As I followed one of the new brooks in a red-maple swamp one autumn day, I came upon a traveling spotted turtle slipping beneath brilliant floats of red and red-orange leaves.

One day I invited my brother John and a friend, Dicky, on an expedition to a more distant marsh, a place of giant reeds and meandering creeks on the outskirts of a saltwater cove farther down the tracks. Hearing a train approaching as we set out, we decided to save some time and energy. We jumped onto the last two boxcars. I had never taken the train very far past the Old Swamp and didn't know that it had different speeds for different runs of track. After crossing a narrow bridge and starting down a straightaway, it began to pick up speed. We looked at one another and down at the crossties and crushed basalt passing faster and faster beneath our feet. With visions of ending up in Providence or Boston and setting an all-time record for being late for supper, I signaled my fellow passengers to jump before the train sped up any more. Leaping as far from the iron wheels and rails as we could, we hit the ground rolling, and we kept on rolling down the steep, gravelly embankment. Picking ourselves up, cut, scraped, and bleeding, we were relieved to find limbs, fingers, and heads intact. Dicky may have been the most relieved, having broken both ankles jumping out of a tree the previous summer.

Though I found new turtle places every summer from age eight to age fourteen, my closest connection was always to my original core of discovery, with the Old Swamp at its heart. This turtle mosaic was complex and mysterious enough to fill long summer days year after year, always seeming to hold another hidden corner here and there. As I reached employable age I began to take on small jobs and paper routes, but if I had a choice between earning money and spending time in the swamps, I went to the swamps. Their hold on me was such that I simply could not stay away, whatever sacrifice I might have to make.

Still surrounded by the overwhelmingly human-centered world that was all I had known for my first eight years, I thought of myself as "Lucky Fox" each time I went off to the swamps. Looking at the lives around me, I told myself over and again, "It doesn't have to be this way . . . there must be another way." I knew that in my turtle revelations I had some luck working for me, had come to insights not widely shared; but I also knew that I had to be ever watchful to dodge the trap, ready to elude the snare. I devoted myself to slipping the noose. I was always on the lookout for openings, as a bird heads for daylight, a salamander for darkness.

Loss

Throughout those first summers of exploring, my turtle world seemed inexhaustible. I thought of it as endless, perhaps because once I entered, my focus became so minutely immediate that I saw no end to my visible universe. But this universe was shrinking, not expanding. On one of the first days of March in my sixth season, I set out for a wet place well downstream from the Old Swamp, where a deeper cut of the brook ran through a seldom flooded, thick red-maple swamp, heavy with shrubs and vines, skunk cabbage and ferns.

The streamside cover was so dense that ducks came here to molt in late summer. And late the previous spring, as I searched the riparian thickets, I had seen across the brook what was almost certainly the rear margin of a big wood turtle's shell. Quickly out of shoes and socks, I waded across and verified my impression. Knowing these turtles only from books, I had dreamed of finding one myself. I did not find another wood turtle that season, and I wondered if the one I did see had been released or had escaped from captivity in the area, or if he was the last of a once thriving colony. New houses and roads had been built not far away, and industrial expansion near the lower run of the brook had eradicated any semblance of wood-turtle habitat.

That beautiful and mysterious sculpted-shelled turtle was on my mind one day the following year as I headed to a spring flood zone along the brook, where a shallow sheet of water drifted slowly through a great thicket of pussy willows—a silvery-catkinned shrub forest at thaw. I went there every March, sometimes as early as late February, to hear the first red-winged blackbirds and cut a few pussy willow branches for my mother. But this day I saw through the red maples not screens and tangles but the unsettling light of open space. I was stunned. There was a great hole in the landscape of the swamp—the landscape of redwings, swamp sparrows, ribbon snakes, pussy willows, and, I had hoped, wood turtles. Where just a year ago so much life had awakened and returned in spring and flourished through summer, bulldozers loomed at the edge of a great muddy plateau they had raised above its lowland surroundings. It would be paved soon enough. I would not be coming back to what was left of the brook. My world—worse, the turtles' world—was contracting. There was not even a place for pussy willows to flower. Numb and in tears at the same time, I learned a new lesson in loss.

About three months later I looked into the face of even more drastic change. On my approach to the Old Swamp I saw a bright yellow shape in the brush—another bulldozer resting, waiting, crouching in a crushed bed of brush. I thought of schemes I had heard about: putting sugar in a gas tank, sand in an engine. But I knew that whatever human design lay behind the sudden intrusion of this instrument of change, I could not stop it, not even with dynamite.

"Things change," I had been hearing. "For the worse," I had been thinking. I had proof, simply by looking around me.

"People gotta have a job and a place to live." This mantra, seemingly unarguable, justified without question or extended thought, had been ringing in my ears. It seemed I could not escape this insistent refrain, nor the annihilation its voracious implementation would wreak on the natural world I had so come to love.

By autumn, trees had been cut down and the earth restructured; the project marched to the borders of the Old Swamp. The sadness of the season's departure that I felt every autumn reached an inconsolable depth. What renaissance could I hope for now in springs to come? The landscape was disappearing and the turtles were being driven into an unforgiving corner. What would become of them? Could they find another place? Could I? I made a visit to the Old Swamp late in leafless autumn. I wore a heavy coat, but still shivered in the chill eastern wind that riffled the gray water. Hard frosts had taken down the green, reedy growth of summer. I needed to go to the swamp even when turtles were sleeping, needed to be where they slept. I had to keep looking into the water even in winter and walk it when it froze. It was all part of the waiting. In previous years, even after frost had thinned the cover, the acres of densely twigged brush had always screened me; now the edge of the swamp was the end of the world; my own cover was being shorn away.

Looking out over the swamp in lowering sunlight, I was surprised to make out a small frog, all but his head covered by a mat of frost-burned bur reed that had slumped into the water. Staring into his unblinking eyes, I thought they must be the last eyes open in the

A song sparrow on a pussy willow branch.

Old Swamp. I imagined the frog felt a shared reluctance to say goodbye to the season. In the water and weeds nothing stirred but the November wind. I kept looking back at the unmoving frog, but he never blinked.

On the verge of a winterlike night, the pale sunlight slipped away. I felt the need to move, to try to warm up a little, but I could not leave the frog. Then, with a sudden rippling, he was gone. I had the strongest feeling I had watched a frog go into hibernation. The reality of the encroachment upon the Old Swamp pressed heavily on my end-of-season emotions, and once again I could not keep back the tears. Not sure how I would honor it, I made a promise to the frog: someday, somehow, I would find a way—I wouldn't let this happen again.

Gordon

One day during the summer between fifth and sixth grade I heard a resounding knock at the screen door of our housing-project duplex, followed by a stentorian voice that announced to my mother: "Mrs. Carroll, my name is Gordon Ultsch. I just moved into town, and I heard that your son is interested in turtles. I study birds, and I think we should get to know one another."

I went out onto the porch to greet a boy my age, a skinnier fellow than his voice had led me to expect, with sandy hair and glasses as thick as the bottom of a Coke bottle. There was an immediate insistence about him; I sensed that in merely stepping out of my house to meet him I had acquired a longtime friend, whether I wanted to or not.

Gordon told me he had been living with his grandparents on Long Island, where he had had some excellent experiences with the eastern box turtles still abundant there at the time. He also knew the famous bird painter Don Eckleberry. Soon after we met I showed him some of my swamps and introduced him to Carr and Pope. Not far into the season I could see that he had been converted from ornithology to herpetology. The next spring he took me to his old stomping grounds on Long Island and introduced me to the incomparably patterned box turtles, which did not occur in my southeastern Connecticut haunts.

He proved more intrepid than I in his interest in the study of amphibians and reptiles. A phone call summoned me to his house one morning. "I've got something to show you, D.C.," he said as he led me to a large aquarium in his backyard. The glass cage was covered with a heavy metal screen weighted down with big stones. It took me a while to make out a pattern in the thick layers of dried grass and leaves: red-brown coils with broad, dark brown spots and wide, black-edged bands that faded to a coppery sienna. He had captured a copperhead. I looked at the motionless snake for a long time, in awe and admiration. I was also awestruck by my friend's having caught a poisonous snake. Sadness entered my emotions later, when Gordon told me that a neighbor who had come to see the copperhead said it should be shot. I urged my friend to release the snake where he had found it, but I wasn't at all sure that my argument won out over the pressure to kill it. I wasn't told, and I never asked about the fate of that remarkably patterned snake.

In junior high we pooled money from our paper routes to subscribe to one of the scientific journals cited in Carr's *Handbook.* We debated between *Copeia* and *Herpetologica,* eventually deciding on the latter because it featured more papers on turtles. We made up our minds that when it was time to go on to college we would somehow get to the University of Florida and study with Archie Carr.

Mr. Moxley and Mr. Malone

In sixth-grade English class, Mr. Moxley assigned us to write a story. I came up with a mystery about a beast with strange tracks, some killings by a large animal that vanished into the forest, which was thought to be some mutant form of wolf but at length proved to be a feral mastiff. After reading the first part of my unfinished tale to the class, he waived my other assigned work so I could keep writing. For a week or more, part of each day's English class was devoted to my reading aloud the latest installment of my ongoing saga, until I finally got to "The End." Mr. Moxley even offered to type my story for me. He was a very big man, and typing wasn't easy for him. As he loomed over the typewriter, which looked like some kind of toy in front of him, he kept hitting two keys at once with his enormous fingers, but he provided me with my first typewritten manuscript.

I did not make a good first impression on Mr. Malone, my seventh-grade science teacher. Although he was to become a great friend and would have a fundamental influence on my life, when he entered his classroom the first day of school he saw me standing on top of my desk, a chair in my hands, jousting with a similarly positioned comrade across the aisle. I was no juvenile delinquent, but I was something of a behavioral work in progress. A tall, thin, older man with a gravelly voice and blazing eyes, Mr. Malone established order at once, without kicking me out of his class.

That inauspicious introduction was put behind us as I quieted down to being an indoor schoolboy for most of the day and applied myself in his stimulating class.

Mr. Malone took me under his wing, and I spent considerable after-school time with him that winter, even spending some weekends at his house in the woods. Gordon came with me on one of those visits, and we searched nearby shallow shrub swamps and seeps for hibernating turtles. We probed into unfrozen pockets here and there with long, thin metal poles, feeling and listening for contact with turtle shells. I had read about this process, called "noodling," which was used by people hunting for snapping turtles for their winter soup pots. Our goal had nothing to do with soup— we just wanted to see if we could find turtles in the wintertime, but we had no luck.

My intimacy with turtles and the wilds was now widely known, and Mr. Malone and some of my other teachers came to my house to see my backyard vivariums, several large enclosures in which I combined ponds featuring sunning stones and mossy banks with dry-land areas of leaf litter, logs, and pieces of bark, making habitats as natural as I could. I filled the vivariums with turtles, snakes, frogs, toads, and salamanders I had found and was keeping for the summer, taking care to separate prey from predators. One time I lifted a pool out to clean it and discovered that a pair of musk turtles had mated, and the female had nested in the dirt right against the side of the pool. I moved the eggs, recreating her shallow nest in a coffee can, and placed it in a warm place next to the hot water tank in the house. When the dime-sized hatchlings appeared in early September, I put parents and little ones back in their native pond.

James Clifford Malone had come to Riverside Elementary from the famous nuclear research center at Oak Ridge, Tennessee. He shared the firm belief of many in that era that nuclear power would be the salvation of mankind, providing free fuel for the world and freeing people physically and creatively to become better beings. Though I was an idealistic youth, I could not quite envision such a future. For the opening of a children's science museum, he arranged for me to give a talk titled "Atomic Theory from Democritus to the Present." I donated my rock collection to this museum, some sixty different rocks identified and labeled.

Early in our friendship Mr. Malone told me he was grooming me for a career in science—specifically, in medicine. To help me publicize my talents so I could get a scholarship to a top university, he encouraged me to undertake a major project for a science competition for New England junior high school students. I decided to research a fungus that infected the shells of tens of thousands of hapless hatchling turtles in the crowded, unclean tanks of dime stores and pet shops. He connected me with researchers at military and industrial installations so that I could use their powerful microscopes and laboratory materials. I took samples from turtle shells, grew the fungus in an agar-agar culture in petri dishes, then isolated and identified it. Experimenting with salt baths, I attempted to find some way to eradicate the fungus, but I was not able to effect a cure.

As the deadline for submission of the projects drew perilously close, my father drove me to a metropolitan post office that had agreed to let us in a back door so that my package could be postmarked a half-hour before midnight. My project won second prize, and a newspaper account, complete with a photo of me receiving the award and a twenty-five-dollar savings bond, reported that I had "discovered" a turtle disease.

The Beach

Our parents occasionally took my younger brother and me to the beach a few miles from our house, where I explored great rock pilings and briny tidal pools and caught little crabs on strings baited with bits of cracked-open mussels. I watched the tiny fish that became stranded in salty depressions scoured in stone by the sea, until it returned to reclaim them. I set up temporary saltwater aquaria with hermit crabs and seaweed in smaller bowls of seawater set in stone. At low tide I searched the sand flats exposed at the base of boulders, looking for sea glass and shells. The plaintive cries of gulls and the murmuring pulse of the tide, whispering on sand, clattering on beds of sea-worn cobble, all had a pull on me. But my fascination was limited. The saltwater shoreline and endless deeps beyond were an alien world. I had no hopes of finding turtles and frogs here. I found the vastness, the colors and forms, the plants and animals of the coastal and marine world, so captivating to many, to be unembraceable; the deep space of the ocean and its unbroken sky only served to turn me inland.

At the dawning of adolescence I spent hours by the sea, drawn back to the beach by its girls, but even then I returned again and again to the world of turtles. Girls, snack bars, and other delights notwithstanding, I would leave the public beach and walk down the road to a fenced-off private one. At the entrance to this seaside club was a long, narrow, brush-bordered water lily pond that abounded in painted turtles. I could crouch among the bushes and watch them paddle lazily about or dart quickly under lily pads if a gull's shadow passed too close. Even though I was at the far end of the pond from the busy entrance gate, I was afraid of being seen if I waded. I always felt extremely uncomfortable if I could be seen while looking for turtles; this feeling led me to seek the most untrodden ways and gave me an empathy for secretive species. Most of the pond was too deep and exposed to view for me to go wading, but, using popcorn as bait, which I tossed ever closer to my hiding place on shore, I lured some of the quick and wary turtles within reach, managing to catch some. Once, at the shallow end of the pond, I just caught sight of a turtle's head going down. Its size and shape, a hint of its color, and its manner of retraction did not signal a painted turtle or any of the other turtles I had come to know.

The lure of the mystery turtle drew me out into the open. I marked the precise site where the turtle's head went down, and did not take my eyes from the spot as I waded toward it. I had to be aware so I could hold still if the turtle resurfaced or track its movements if it took off. If I looked away even momentarily, it would be very difficult to relocate that precise point in the pond-covering flotillas of lily pads. I felt my way among sunken stones and pockets of mud with my feet so that I never had to look away from the spot I had targeted—basic skills I had begun to evolve in my earliest turtle stalkings.

The water was only knee-deep where I had seen the mystery turtle, so getting to the site was easier than I had expected. As I groped beneath the lily pads, my fingertips touched down on the broad dome of her shell. I could tell at once that this turtle was bigger than any painted turtle, and I knew from the glimpse of her head that she was not a snapping turtle. I gripped her with both hands and lifted her from the water. Her carapace was deep green and gray-green, barred with yellow, all these colors edged with black. She was a female red-eared slider, the ubiquitous species of pet shops and dime stores.

Was she a hatchling pet who had been released and had survived to adulthood in the mild climate of coastal Connecticut, hundreds of miles north of her natural range? Or was she one of those few of the tens of thousands of pet turtles who did not die within a year or two in captivity but lived so long and grew so large that her owner decided to release her? Unable to resist the temptation to keep this unusual turtle, I carried her home to become a spectacular, unfortunately outsized denizen of one of my outdoor vivaria for a time.

Down the road from the lily pond was another large pond. It had no water lilies, but the rock-studded open water at the center was ringed with marshes and backwaters. Looking through the chain-link fence surrounding it, I could see painted turtles basking on the

A painted turtle among lily pads.

rocks. The fence was hung with forbidding signs denoting the interior of a military post and warning against entry. But the pond, with its swaths of emergent grasses and dense colonies of tussock sedge, portended spotted turtles as well.

One day Gordon and I decided to try to get into the pond. We followed the imposing fence to where it ran through dense woods that hid us from the road. Trees pressing close against the fence aided us in scaling it. Once inside we waded into the warm shallow water, keeping to weedy borders where spotted turtles would be likely to hide.

The bottom was soft and muddy, the water murky. I was feeling for turtles with my feet when a shot rang out and a spray of pellets hit the water not far from us. No one appeared; no one yelled at us. No one had to—we splashed out of the pond, grabbed our shoes, and raced through the trees. As we scaled the fence, a second shot rang out and pellets shredded the leaves of nearby trees. I was always the worst at climbing fences, but with this motivation I kept up with Gordon pretty well in going over the top. I was only shot at one other time in my life, in the autumn of the same year, while doing some nocturnal fruit-picking with friends in an apple and pear orchard.

Bill and DeDe

The first day of my freshman year in high school, Mr. Miller, the art teacher, said, "Art is the only thing that lasts. Civilizations come and go, governments do not really matter. All that endures is the art that people do."

This heretical pronouncement, which ran counter to much of what I had been hearing for fourteen years, struck a deep chord in me. I ran it by my mother when I got home from school. I sensed from her guarded look and lack of spoken response that she saw a new potential for trouble ahead.

Mr. Miller seemed to teach without teaching, imparting only the necessary instructions with consummate minimalism. He was a painter and a sculptor, but I rarely saw any of his own artwork. His teaching was his art; his students, his medium. He recognized genius in many forms and sometimes saw it in students other teachers would not take a second look at. He didn't follow a lesson plan. He simply found and fostered talent, letting it evolve. In his classroom that year I began to understand what it meant to be an artist and to adopt the life of an artist. My talent for drawing and painting had been recognized when I was very young—from first grade on I was one of those who got to decorate school bulletin boards for various holidays, and my work was a regular feature of display cabinets— but I had never really had *art* before I met Mr. Miller. I had had art classes, but I had never had art. From the day I entered his art room, art and life, my life in and out of the swamps, became intermingled, inseparable.

Even by art studio standards his room was legendary for its lack of order. But its profound disarray was a fertile clutter, as rich in possibilities for expansion as the Devonian sea. He was not entirely without standards and would say to an incoming class, "Please don't hang your coats on the floor." His art room, the antithesis of my father's dictum "A place for everything and everything in its place" quickly became a home to me.

"Even God had to have chaos before he could create," I heard Mr. Miller say to a teacher who was looking in from the doorway, her face the picture of astonishment.

Our first project in art class was to make a handbound book. We were to choose the paper, sew the folded sheets into signatures, and bind them into a cloth-covered volume of blank pages. We could illustrate our pages however we wanted.

I did a painting of a swamp on my first page, in black watercolor and India ink, with highlights of opaque white gouache. It showed black trees and vines with gray boulders, gray sky, black water, with wan washes and sharper glimmerings of white. This outwardly lugubrious scene might have prompted some teachers to schedule a session for me with the school counselor, or at least to suggest that I find a watercolor set with something besides black in it. But to me the painting was an intimation not of gloom and despair but of hope and rebirth. Rising from gray and white slicks of water on black mud at the base of a great twisted grapevine was a spear of spring green blushed with crimson, a skunk cabbage thrusting forth at winter's end. I knew that when this hardy plant appeared, spotted turtles would not be far behind. On a foldout from the watercolor page I lettered a prose poem on the coming of spring and some rhymed couplets in praise of skunk cabbage.

All through high school I continued to work on my book. I painted watercolors of sunsets over waterways and pastures; a sentinel stand of grass by the edge of the sea; woods. I did a pen-and-ink landscape with the distant silhouette of a lone figure on a hill, accompanied by a poem devoted to lost love. There was also a pen-

The swamp at thaw, from my first handbound book.

and-ink study of the Old Swamp, drawn from memory. I painted a watercolor of a small northern brown snake, arabesquely poised in leaves and twigs, bits of his native habitat I had collected to keep with my subject in a glass bowl while I did my study from life. Beside the painting I wrote a poem about a snake just emerging from hibernation.

A northern brown snake, from my first handbound book.

Mr. Miller and I became close friends. In the spring of that first year he took me to his house to meet his wife, DeDe, and their six-month-old daughter. His house mirrored the agreeable chaos of his art room. Only after a lengthy and conscientious relocation of layers of papers, books, prints, records, and art supplies was there an empty chair to sit in. If my teacher's classroom was the setting of an awakening, his house was an arena of enlightenment. DeDe quickly became a friend as well, a mentor in her own way. Together the Millers became integral to my life and work. Students were frequent visitors at their house, but over the course of my high school years I was nearly a resident.

Mr. Miller was the first person I met who moved more slowly than I did. Though a dedicated gardener, he had no particular affinity with the outdoor natural world; but to me there seemed to be something of the turtle in him. He possessed what I thought of as an Indian or Mexican sense of time . . . there was always time. He had in fact lived in Mexico and still owned a house there. Though nowhere near as fluent as he, I spoke Spanish with him and often thought of going to Mexico or elsewhere in Latin America. Inspired by William Henry Hudson's romantic *Green Mansions, The Purple Land,* and other writings, I imagined that I might be driven to find my last wild places there, my "Uruguayan option."

Process was more important than completion to my teacher, and his house epitomized this, ever being extended in all four directions. He told me he never wanted to finish building it, and in fact he never did. The summer after my freshman year he hired me to help him pour a concrete footing for a fieldstone fireplace and a studio at the back of the house, which was actually a relocated unit from a housing project like the one I lived in. I was not known for my zeal in seeking jobs, but I was eager to work with Bill and had my father drop me off there early the first day. The Millers were still asleep.

I walked in the woods for a while and found them stirring when I returned.

"DeDe thinks we should have some breakfast before we go to work," Bill said. "She's going to make blueberry pancakes . . . Would you like to come help me pick the blueberries?"

He took up one container and handed me another, and we set off into the woods that surrounded their house.

Cedar Pastures

During the first spring I knew them, the Millers told me about a pond across the road from their house. Crossing the road, I climbed over a stone wall and slipped into a brushy thicket studded with oak and hickory trees. As I crept up to the pond, I felt at once the intimations of wildness that stirred within me whenever I found a new wild place. Thick and black, three great water snakes lay closely coiled on a rock near the shore. Through a screen of shrubs they looked like an old tire. I circled away so as not to disturb them, then emerged at the water's edge and stood up. Another large water snake dropped heavily into the water from an overhanging branch, and several painted turtles scrambled from their basking place at a far corner of the pond.

The pond was man-made, with a dam and a standpipe. But the land around it, once pasture, had gone back to forest. Beavers had long ago disappeared from coastal Connecticut, but plants and animals had colonized the abandoned human-dug pond as readily as they would have a beaver impoundment. I colonized it myself to an extent; it became my new place to swim with turtles, and with water snakes as well. In warm weather I took off my clothes and became a part of the pond life. As I swam in the cool bottom water one hot summer day I saw a painted turtle speeding away from me. I overtook the turtle, caught him, and brought him to the surface for a moment, the only time I ever sighted, pursued, and captured a turtle underwater without the aid of swim fins or diving mask.

The pond did not appear to be likely habitat for spotted turtles. The emergent sedges and shrubs were restricted to a very narrow fringe, with a sudden drop to relatively deep, open water. It was a fine environment for water snakes, frogs, and painted turtles, but spotted turtles nearly always keep to broader, shallower depths with heavy vegetative cover.

The Millers had also mentioned an abandoned farm property down a wooded lane with a few houses along it. After my initiation in the pond, I set off for the old farm, with a great sense of expectation. At the end of the lane, the woods dropped off to an open expanse of saltmarsh bordering a narrow cove. A stream entered the tidal marsh from the woods, fresh water returning to the sea. Heavy clumps of tall grass lined the upland edge, a screen of giant reeds stood off in one marshy backwater. The low saltmarsh grasses were golden in early spring, and beyond were black mud flats exposed by low tide and the sharp blue water of the inlet. Long oak ridges rose to the east of the estuary; to the west, on low, rolling knolls, stood red cedars in large fields marked off by stone walls. These unmown pastures were grown in with tufted grasses, a ground of palest straw gold scattered with the dark cedars.

I followed a dirt road inland toward the low hills. I passed a great barn with wide doors fallen away and massive timbers beginning to sag, yielding to the workings of the seasons and the insistence of gravity. The great smooth-cut blocks of the granite foundation did not yet show any sign of surrendering to these inexorable forces. I walked along high ground a short distance to a parting of the ways. The main fork, with its well-worn wheel ruts, led on to a higher hill that had outcrops of ledge and occasional open lots of former pasture framed by stone walls. The lesser fork was a darker trail, more animal path than wagon road. It sloped to wetter ground and uncut woods, red maple swamp and dense shrub thicket. If there were turtles here, this trail would take me to them.

A chorus of spring peepers came drifting up from the swamp, a song to heighten my hopes that I was on the track of spotted turtles. The footing became wetter, the trail narrowed. The damp path was bordered by highbush blueberry shrubs of surprising stature. Ancient-looking monuments of their kind, they were twisted and contorted, with the serpentine grace of the most picturesque mountain pines of Chinese scrolls and Japanese screen paintings. I ran my fingers along their rough-barked writhings. Although the saturated soil they stood on held no standing water, their presence heightened my expectations. Skunk cabbage had already spread broad swaths in the muddier places. Its wide, spring-green leaves held thousands of little crimson flowers that had fallen from the upper swamp canopy of red maples. The time of the red maples' flowering, from bud break to setting of seed, is a signal time for the spotted turtle and my favorite season within the seasons.

Moving to low ground, feeling the earth, reading the vegetation, using my senses of sight and smell, and calling upon some vague guiding intuition, I was seeking a way to water that might hold spotted turtles. I still didn't know the names of all the plants of swamp and marsh, but I knew them as plants of turtle places, and the ones around me I knew as the vegetation of spotted turtle neighborhoods. My knowledge of nature was still largely aboriginal, very much learned in the field.

I made my way toward a screen of alders and red maples rising above a haze of bud-breaking brush and glimpsed a silvery reflection through dark stems of alder and a smoke of twigs, April light on April water. I stalked up to a long, narrow pool of clear spring rain collected over a dark floor of leaves, open water so clear it looked as if it had just dropped from the sky. The channel curled out of sight in the surrounding thicket.

The northern fringe of the pool was lined with boulders, the southern margin ridged with tipped-up root mounds of wind-thrown maples. Or had these trees been pushed over by some other means? The troughlike pool, a little over a foot deep at full flood, appeared man-made, perhaps bulldozer-made. Whatever the ditch's original purpose, it had become a seasonal pond filled by autumn and winter rains and recolonized by swamp vegetation. If there were spotted turtles in the area, they would surely track their way to the pool much as I had, but with knowledge and senses far keener than mine. They would colonize it just as water snakes and painted turtles had the dug pond I had discovered about an hour and a half before. With all the surrounding habitat, this would be as good as a glacier-gouged pool to spotted turtles. I came upon a garter snake coiled in dry leaves not far from the water's edge, taking the late slants of sun exactly as I had seen spotted turtles do.

A brilliant spotted turtle.

The spotted-turtle search-image I carried as I scanned the leaf-littered shore did not become reality, but another picture I held in my mind, of one resplendent in clear water, was fulfilled almost too soon to believe. As I slipped around a boulder, in a strikingly precise fit to anticipation, I saw a spotted turtle, perfectly still, looking up at me from sunken leaf litter in perfectly still water. Landscape with turtle . . . Once again a turtle at its center brought the landscape all the more to life to me. The way he held still, with his eyes trained in my direction led me to think that the turtle had anticipated me, though I did not know how he could have sensed me as I circled behind the big stone.

"They are here," I found myself whispering to the stones, the trees, the pool. Not only was the season here, with singing frogs, flowering red maples, unfurling skunk cabbage, and budding alders, but spotted turtles were here. For a long time I looked at the unmoving turtle. A wind shivered across the pool, a few more red maple flowers fell to its surface. A robin's evensong lilted out of the bordering wooded swamp, and the chorusing of spring peep frogs came up anew. I felt that I had come home again.

As I concluded my search of the pool I glimpsed ahead the reflection of another ponding in a low skunk-cabbage hollow under red maples. Like the first one, this seasonal waterhold had an aggregation of spotted salamander eggs and several complements of wood-frog eggs. No turtle. Next I came to a pool barely twelve feet in diameter, set among stones, some sixteen inches deep, with a thick layer of sunken leaves and underwater branches heavily hung with egg clutches of spotted salamanders. No turtle here either; but each of these ponds held the promise that a spotted turtle, bearing its orange head blazings and signature constellation of spots, might appear at any time.

I had found a new turtle world. I had already established a pattern in my life, adopted from my early days in the Old Swamp, when I would keep to a hummock until just before it went under, then leap to another until it began to sink, of trusting that I could always make my way to another place. I entered this new world with an open heart and bonded with it as wholly as I had that first turtle backwater. The possibility that this place, too, might disappear never entered my mind. Perhaps, in order to be here the way I needed to be, I had to come into it from pure belief.

As I walked back out, I turned up the trail to higher ground. Coming around again to make my descent, I saw tall willows off in the lowland. In the light of a spring afternoon fading to evening, I wrestled my way to them through the toughest tangle I had yet encountered. A shadowy cottontail lolloped just out of reach and settled down in a thorny grove, chewing, watching. As I had hoped, the willows led me to another pool, bouldered at one end and thicketed round about, with a small stand of giant reeds and a corner of emergent pussy willows. I kept still long enough for the peepers to resume their calling. A small, stealthy flock of red-winged blackbirds and grackles appeared in brush close by and took up a musically raucous serenade, a talking in tongues I let myself think I could understand in part. I surrendered my ears to the frogs and birds but kept my eyes on the water. A spotted turtle emerged from sunken reeds, perfectly visible for a moment, sliding along the bottom, then turned out of sight into one of the black caves among the stones.

Upon leaving, I cut some pussy willows, which were full-blown, well beyond the favored compact, silvery stage. But wound with a few wisps of dried sedge they made a fine bouquet, the first of many I would bring to DeDe at the conclusion of a sojourn in this new realm of the turtles.

For four years I kept a steady round of the seasons here. In spring and summer, I came at every chance, especially when heavy rains had refilled the pools, making it likely that I would find spotted turtles. My route followed a circuit I had mapped out in my mind as I discovered the pools. There were small, marshy depressions, little more than shin-deep even in the wettest seasons; pockets of seasonal shrub swamp; and a more extensive deep-muck, heavily thicketed fen that bordered one large permanent pond. Each pool had its own distinctive arrangement of water and plants, but all had in common the sun-speckled turtles that moved among them. These waterholds constituted only a fraction of the upland landscape in which they were hidden, and within them were hidden occasional painted and snapping turtles but, far more often, spotted turtles. I found hatchlings, young ones, adults; I found them at the edge of thin ice in the first meltwater, in little cattail pockets when redwings sang, in shallow, watery depressions with rose pogonia orchids not long after summer solstice, in hurricane-flooded lacings of cranberry in late summer and autumn. Once again the spotted turtle had led me to a landscape that I was compelled to be in even during summer's drought and winter's cold, the turtles' time of hiding and hibernation. Through these children of the sun's dialogue with the earth I could continue to pass out of human time and place and enter the soul of the seasons.

I found this place, which I called Cedar Pastures, alone, and I kept to it alone. Solitude and silence intensified my seeing; they were integral to my experience of the place. Though I went more frequently from mid-March into July, when the spotted turtles were most active, I roamed this landscape throughout the seasons. Even in high summer, when most of the pools dried up and the spotted turtles dug out of sight, I went again and again. I moved along to catbird calls, when the stones of the walls were still warm to the touch even hours after sunset. I heard the sharp, clear whistles of bobwhite by day, whip-poor-will calls by night. Taking trails of the deer and the fox, I loped down from high pastures, sometimes following a fox who was just beginning his nocturnal rounds. Well aware of me, he would trot just ahead in the waning light, not forsaking his path, keeping a constant distance between us that evidently freed him of fear of me, until he turned off into rabbit-hiding tangles at an appointed place along his route. Below the uplands, veeries sang at dusk, their spiraling calls blurred in their own echoing as light blurred in the imprecise landscape of the darkening hollows. In May and June the wet lowlands were sweet with swamp azaleas. Their final perfumed flowering mingled with the first spicy blooming of sweet pepperbush, which lay heavy on the humid air long into summer. The scents of the swamp thickets deepened in evening air as night came on to replace the intoxication of twilight, and pale wraiths of mist rose up and drifted among them.

Sometimes, after the time of foxes setting forth and the first moths fluttering, I would stay on in the dark and await the moon, then walk the moon-bright open fields and feel my way through ink-shadowed stands of oak. I kept still in fringes of dark moon shadow and watched as fox and skunk hunted in their different ways, almost within my reach. When I walked along the crest of a high ledge I often saw deer move silent and shadowlike through an orchard of aged apple trees below. I took to animal trails that wound through the descending chain of pastures bright with lunar light, in which Druid trees were gathered, red cedars black in the pale glow, standing in silent gatherings and processions stopped in their tracks. I almost expected to hear their voices in the night, see them move in the moonlight. Unhinged by time, moon-bleached gates opened invitingly at breaks in the glowing gray walls of stone. So

The highland trail, Cedar Pastures.

different, the twilight time of bat and fox, of shadow-deer and flitting moths, and the later dark, with its sky full of stars all suns too far away, from the time of turtles, bright day with its one star burning, the other half of time in the same summer world.

By day I walked higher pastures of low silky grass that went lavender in autumn. I roved fields of bronzy grass set with deep orange clusters of butterflyweed and followed stone walls edged with blueberry and sumac, tree lines of black cherry and an occasional black gum. I dodged greenbrier and brushed through sweetfern and bayberry until my hair and clothing smelled of them. In the company of standing cedars, I sat at stone tables in all four seasons.

Walden

In eleventh-grade English, we were handed a book that I had never heard of: Henry David Thoreau's *Walden*. From the opening paragraph, I was transfixed. The very idea of this book—its reason for being, its empathy with nature and view of human society—electrified me.

Reading some paragraphs was like finding fragments of my own turtle world come to life between the covers of a book. I could taste his descriptions of the pondside, the marshes and swamps, fields and woods, light and seasons, his world just enough apart from the world of man to be the realm of nature.

By the time I read "How many a man has dated a new era in his life from the reading of a book!" I knew I could date a new era in my life from my reading of Thoreau. It was new not in the sense of a departure in a previously unknown direction but in affirmation, broadened revelation, deepened resolve. I found myself, as one of my favorite quotes from Robert Frost went, "only more sure of all I thought was true."

Also, Thoreau's critiques of his Yankee neighbors and their society backed up my arguments with the physical, economic, and spiritual human constructs pressing in on me from all sides. To me the issues he raised were current and unresolved, only intensified by the passage of time and proliferation of people.

> I have traveled a good deal in Concord; and everywhere, in shops, and offices, and fields, the inhabitants have appeared to me to be doing penance in a thousand remarkable ways ... The twelve labors of Hercules were trifling in comparison with those which my neighbors have undertaken; for they were only twelve, and had an end ...
>
> Our manners have been corrupted by communication with the saints. Our hymn-books resound with a melodious cursing

Avenues of sunlight along watery ditches.

of God and enduring Him forever. One would say that even the prophets and redeemers had rather consoled the fears than confirmed the hopes of man . . .

I embraced this radical treatise, this manifesto grounded in wildness. Quotes from *Walden* began to pepper my speech, prompting my mother to exclaim one day, "That damn Thoreau and Bill Miller!"

But in my own devotion to becoming lost in and absorbed by my wild-as-possible surroundings, I was not prone to Thoreauvian philosophical musings. It seemed that he went looking for lofty thoughts where I went looking for turtles. I felt at home in his book in a way that was curiously akin to how I felt at home with the turtles.

In walking the long days' avenues of sunlight along watery ditches by the railroad tracks, wading among the blueberry mounds and shrub thickets of the red-maple swamp, crouching in giant reeds beside spotted-turtle channels just upstream from the pulse of the tides, I felt that I was living the kind of time that permeates *Walden*. To paraphrase its author, time was but the stream I went a-turtling in.

> My days were not the days of the week, bearing the stamp of any heathen deity, nor were they minced into hours and fretted by the ticking of a clock; for I lived like the Puri Indians, of whom it is said that "for yesterday, to-day and to-morrow they have only one word, and they express the variety of meaning by pointing backward for yesterday, forward for to-morrow, and overhead for the passing day."

I would cleave to that sense of time in a world running counter to the direction of my dreams.

Art, Biology, Writing

In senior English class I ventured away from poetry, prose poems, and essays into forms as diverse as satire and the short story. As a reader I have never had much liking for short stories, but my one attempt at writing one, "The Fox," won honorable mention in the Scholastic Writing Awards contest. I had expected a better chance of recognition in the Scholastic Art Awards, but this did not happen. I thrived in the humanities aura in my school at that time, an intermingling of art, science, literature, foreign language, and other disciplines, in a most stimulating and encouraging setting. I was released from art classes to rehearse for plays and to work on stage sets. Telling me I was well ahead in my classwork, my English teacher often let me skip his class and go to the art room. Mr. Miller would open the side door and let me drift out into the surrounding fields and woods. Sometimes I would write rather than draw or paint. One day I returned at the end of class to show Mr. Miller a poem I had just written, entitled "Thinking, Just Thinking."

"What!" he exclaimed in mock horror, "You spent my whole art class 'thinking, just thinking'?"

My biology teacher commissioned me to paint a mural, in oils, depicting the history of medicine on a panel three feet high by fifteen feet long. My opening scene was an eye-catching, if not Sistine ceiling–quality, depiction of Stone Age trepanning. One had to assume this procedure was reserved for only the most severe headaches. The patient was held on the ground while a doctor wielding a sharpened split of bone and a pounding stone drilled beneficial holes in his skull. Medicine had a long way to go in fifteen feet.

I had not worked much in oil paints up to that point, and to my eye the mural had an on-the-job-training look to it. Mr. Miller thought it a wonderful demonstration of my rapid progress as an oil painter. At first I found the demonstration a bit painfully public, and I didn't see my progress as being all that rapid. But by the time

I got to the Bubonic Plague I had mastered my medium well enough to portray a pretty gripping scene: well-rendered rats loomed large in the foreground, cartloads of bodies were being dumped into a common grave in the middle ground, and a medieval city towered in the distance. I chipped away at this epic from the latter part of Biology One through Advanced Biology and the end of high school. I don't recall that I got much past Louis Pasteur.

I continued to sense a disparity between biology as taught in school and nature as I had come to know it through the seasons of the turtles. The book-and-lab class had no real connection with my outdoor world. I had a keen enough interest in the school subject, particularly the classification of organisms and the concept of evolution, but as I worked on dissecting a sheep's head with my lab mate Alma, taking it from its vat of formaldehyde day after day, I found I preferred living heads, with eyes that could look back at me from the swamps and marshes.

At final exam time, lingering thoughts of an academic career in biology were put to rest. Advanced Bio was the last period of the day. As the teacher passed out what we all knew would be the mother of all finals, he announced with his trademark chuckle that of course his exam could not be completed within the time allotted for a single class, and he advised us to disregard the day-ending bell and figure on catching the late bus.

I raised my hand and delivered a brief statement to the effect that final exams were supposed to be completed within regular class time. I didn't express the corollary that during turtle season my afterschool hours were especially critical.

"I didn't say anyone had to stay after school, I simply said that no one could expect to complete this test within the class period and get a passing grade."

When the bell rang I alone gathered up my books, went to the front of the room, and placed my test paper on the teacher's desk. He looked up in silence, then went back to his writing. The class took several seconds from their sweat-inducing mental labors to watch me as I walked out. I received an F on the final, bringing what had been an A down to a D.

A little over a month before, I had traveled to Boston to submit a portfolio of my artwork as application for admission to the School of the Museum of Fine Arts. It was my sole college application. A prominent feature of my portfolio, one that I hoped would lead to acceptance, was my first handbound book.

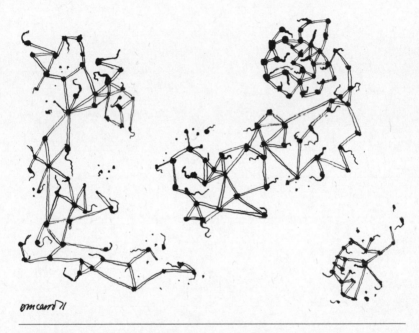

ART SCHOOL

The eye is the meeting place of many roads.

—Paul Klee

My Room

AFTER MY FATHER helped me carry the last of my possessions into the rooming house on Westland Avenue in Boston, then got into his car and headed back to Connecticut, I went from being a wader of turtled swamps and marshes to being a walker of peopled streets and buildings.

Now a student at the Museum School, I had my books, a few art supplies, paper and pens, a radio, and a spotted turtle. My first-floor room had a bed, three chairs (the same number Thoreau had in his cabin), a table, and a closet. Two tall, narrow windows looked out at a five-story, windowless brick wall across an alley. I could see the orangey Back Bay glow of the late afternoon sun high on the wall and the shadow play of neighboring buildings, but the sunlight never made its way into my room. Incremental enactments of the sun's setting played out on the screen of that brick wall over the course of the seasons. The view held intimations of light and time and of the nostalgia I found so compelling in the paintings of the surrealist painter Giorgio de Chirico, one of the artists whose work was beginning to inspire me.

During my long days in the Museum School studios I was a draftsman and painter, putting pencil to paper and brush to canvas. During my hours in my room I was a writer; long scrolls filled with minute handwriting went to Bill and DeDe several times a week, another stream of letters went to scattered friends and my family at home. I kept a copious journal in a script that bordered on being microscopic.

On many nights I walked the streets for hours, covering many miles. Time mattered no more to me in these nocturnal wanderings than it had when I walked along the train tracks and brooks and waded the swamps of my boyhood. I still did not own a watch. From evening until the early morning hours I wandered, celebrating my freedom and solitude, my loneliness.

The financial district was utterly deserted at night and surprisingly dark in the middle of the bright city; everything was closed up, as though money needed to sleep after a tempestuous day of being traded. I walked through a skyscraper forest of polished marble and steel, at the base of cliffs of dark glass.

I walked from the Back Bay across the Charles River to Cambridge, sometimes all the way to Harvard Square. I followed the starlike street lights of the Massachusetts Avenue bridge and strolled in parks along the river where human figures, not deer, moved like shadows in lamplight rather than moonlight. Sometimes I did not get back to my room until two or three in the morning, but I was still ready the next day for the studio-world at school.

I went out to walk in every one of the infrequent Boston snow-falls. Nobody else seemed to be afoot on snowy nights, and the endless parade of cars fell off to an occasional passing. Snow silenced my surroundings, seemed to hold everything still. At two o'clock one December morning I went out in snow that had begun in the early evening. I saw not a soul, heard not a sound, as I walked through the ankle-deep drifts in the streets. At a vacant lot I dug out some branches trimmed from trucked-in Christmas trees, shook them free of snow, and brought them back to my room, where I formed them into a solstice-tree.

I walked in the rain too, warm rain or cold. Like the snow, it magnified what I could feel of the season in this urban environment and muted the extraneous and antagonistic. Day and night, temperature and precipitation—these elements made up the structure of the seasons in the city and imparted some of the heart and soul of seasons I had come to know in the swamps to my vastly different new world.

The Fens

The great green doors of the Museum School opened out to the Fenway. Across this tree-lined paved thoroughfare lay the Fens, and through this urban greenbelt meandered the Muddy River, a sluggish brown waterway adrift with mementos of city life, whose turbid colloidal flow moved over deep sediments composed of God knows what.

I ranged the river banks, some of them shaven and shorn, others fringed with brush and marshy vegetation, and lingered among the great twisted trunks of ancient black willow and luxurious stands of giant reeds. People tended to keep to the wide, open paths and the bridges, at least by day. Leaning against the deeply furrowed bark of a willow's sinuous ascent, lodging myself between a tree and the reedy water's edge, I could go unnoticed and find a measure of solitude in the midst of the multitude. During one of my leanings I was startled by movement in the water, which I did not expect to find inhabited by anything but the half-tame ducks on its surface. Staring into the muddy tea, I began to make out fish-forms, the shapes and slow stirrings of big carp, olive and bronzy brown in the murky shallows. Some appeared to be three feet long. Smaller golden and red-orange ones, former residents of many an apartment goldfish bowl, I suspected, were invisible, in spite of their brilliance, until they rose close to the surface. At times the carp cruised or hovered with their backs out of the water. There were no frogs, no dragonflies or water plants that I could see; the voracious and ever-mouthing fish, as well as the nature of the water they kept forever turbid, suppressed any possibility for biodiversity.

In the Fens I watched sunsets through screens of willow branches, over the cutout shapes of buildings blue in shadow, warm brick orange in sunlight—rectangular hills and ridges, landscape silhouettes shaped by human geometry. In the last of the afternoon sun, I drowsed on grassy slopes a few yards from the endless stream of people going by. Solitude came with the closing of my eyes. Absorbed in their own worlds, seemingly unaware of grass and singing crickets, people were not there to me as they walked by. The murmuring sounds of the city were overlaid by ceaseless cricket song—crickets being one constant as my world changed. Voices seemed far away, and the steady sounds of traffic, accented by automobile horns, seemed more distant than the street that spawned them.

Following the muddy water, I came to somewhat wilder places. I had to work at finding wildness here and needed help from my imagination to see it. I often went to the Victory Gardens, where I was struck by the intermingling of vegetables and flowers in the *abbondanza* of the Italians' small plots. I hoped to emulate the diversity of these city gardens in my own plantings someday, though with subtler colorings in the flowers. A few of the less well attended gardens ran wild with asters and goldenrod, heavy with narcotized bees sipping the varied nectars of the opiate urban flowerland.

Beyond the gardens, footpaths, and mown swards were tall grasses going to seed and more unkempt drifts of wildflowers edging the broad belts of river-keeping reeds. Even in Boston I could slip through screens and pass unnoticed, if not invisible. In the willows and brushy tangles, in the soggy footing under giant reeds, some flocks of migrant birds and I found seclusion.

Late one afternoon, as I made my way along the water's edge to a wider section of the Muddy River, I saw sunlight glinting on the shells of turtles basking on mats of fallen stems surrounding emergent stands of reed some distance from shore. They looked too big to be painted turtles but were too far away for me to identify. And I saw no way to get a closer look. Perhaps I could borrow binoculars someday.

In spring the gold-greening of the willows and the blue shadows of early morning and late afternoon on buildings became my "Bare Willows and Distant Mountains," an urban variation of the exquisitely evocative landscape on silk by Ma Yuan that I went so often to see in the Chinese painting galleries of the Museum of Fine Arts. Bright forsythia, though not native and too rigidly set along walkways and severely shaped by pruning, nonetheless insisted on cheering my heart. Sometimes near the water I found budding and blooming branches left by the gardeners who kept the Rose Garden and its surroundings trimmed. I carried an armload of bright gold forsythia to my room and did a study of the bushlike bouquet in pen and brown ink.

There were no alder thickets or velvet-mossed blueberry and red-maple islands in the Muddy River, but leaning out over the imperceptibly drifting water from a secure hold in the willows, looking into it as I so often used to in swamps and along brooks, I could make out turtle shells. Small and stonelike, they had a green-brown, slatey tone close to the color of the river. These were musk turtles, survivors from the more abundant and diverse wildlife of the original fens, living on in the city unseen and, I am certain, unknown. Unmoving, clasping sunken limbs, their carapaces barely beneath the surface in sunstruck backwaters, they basked in underwater sunlight. Straining my eyes, I could make out their pointed heads, even the thin, light yellow stripes running along the head. Chins resting on the sunken logs they clung to, the motionless turtles perfected their imitation of bumps on a log.

During my second autumn I found a second native turtle species, a hatchling snapping turtle settled in mud among reeds. I suspected he had recently completed his nest-to-water journey, and I wondered whether the muddy shallows would be sheltering enough. Carp were swimming nearly half out of water, all but bellying onto shore in their eagerness to forage. But this little turtle, who still bore his egg tooth, had parents somewhere in this murky channel. Snapping turtles persisted, and musk turtles must also be breeding here in this sluggish river teeming with large fish who would feed on just about anything. And the shorelines were rampant with rats even less fastidious about what they chewed up. At least one native turtle-chewing predator stalked the muddy embankments as well. One night as I walked the Fens I saw a small snow of feathers swirling to the ground. Looking up into a tree through its leafy cover in the city's nocturnal sky glow, I made out a raccoon plucking a pigeon.

With the exception of the musk and snapping turtles, the

species I began to find here were nonnative turtles liberated, like the goldfish, from apartment aquaria. It was sad yet intriguing that I never knew what I'd pull forth when I followed turtle movements in the muddy waters . . . all sorts of sliders, map turtles, western and southern painted turtles, the stock of the pet trade. In the more roughly vegetated terrain beyond the Victory Gardens I found a Florida box turtle and a gopher tortoise. It didn't seem likely that any of these exotics could survive the Boston winters—or so I thought until I managed to work my way to a vantage point where I could verify the identities of the sun-reflecting shells I had seen from afar, back in September. As I had begun to suspect, they were not eastern painted turtles but red-eared sliders. Seeing them in autumn and then again in the same place the following spring convinced me that this species overwintered here; they had probably even established a breeding colony in Boston, as they had in several other places well outside their species' natural range. I thought back to the large red-eared slider I had found as a boy, in a lily pond by the sea in Connecticut. With its natives and transplants, the Fens would be my landscape with turtles for now.

Girls

From a strange distance one girl in a studio class caught my eye and my imagination. For the first two years of art school she was ever on my mind. We came close at moments. Over a number of classes I surreptitiously did a drawing of her, a little at a time, as she worked at her drawing board. I drew another portrait in my journal:

> April 13: She is delicate, her tiny hands are vases for flowers. The quiet beauty of her face and the softness of her sleepy eyes hide in the fullness of the long, light hair that surrounds them. Her head is often turned away in slight avoidance, timid but not uneasy. Her silent lips spread easily into warmth but seldom

part . . . What words she does speak are as evasive as her appear-ance. In the unchanging tranquility of her face, her eyes offer no sign other than mystery. She is her own closely guarded secret.

Her body hides in her clothes, as her mind hides in her gray-green eyes. The softness with which her dress falls over her shoulders, small breasts, and slender waist is borne with an ease to complement her face. Cloaked in a cloud, she cannot be found.

Often the girl stands at a window, a doe gazing into the for-est, with the sun in the warmth of her hair reflecting along her face and slender neck, her face aslant, looking off. A short time and she is gone . . . the doe is among dark trees. She is always just about to leave, ever on her way somewhere, always with a coat on, going out a door.

The female nude came to the fore in my drawings: woman as art and idea, dream and desire, both in my studio figure studies and in the sketchbooks I filled from memory and imagination. I found an embodiment of the romantic-erotic ideal in Picasso's sublime drawings and etchings on the theme of the artist and his model . . . I would have such an atelier. As in my younger school days, I primar-ily sought the company of girls; I had a tendency to idealize them and seemed especially attracted to the elusive ones.

My most constant companion in my first two years at art school gave me a lavishly illustrated volume on the painting and writing of Paul Klee. She had received it as a gift herself, but in her inscription Becky wrote "He is your God, not mine." More directly than most Western artists, Paul Klee addressed the inward vision, the link be-tween the eye and the mind, and saw that to be a painter one must be a philosopher. I gave Becky a handbound book of my poems.

One girl, whom I called "my little sparrow," attracted me by her intensity, her green eyes flashing with emotion. In the midst of an unhappy engagement, she told me she never wanted to belong to anybody or to have anybody belong to her.

Some girls I knew only from the parties that were a regular

feature of one circle I traveled in. They were not part of my world at school, and those I was close to in the art-studio world did not enter this circle.

I was drawn to a dark-haired, dark-eyed one, and I walked her to her apartment on a couple of occasions when we happened out the Museum School doors at the same time. But even at such a small school we were on different paths, paths that rarely crossed. In the spring of our first year, we met by chance near our lockers in the school basement and became involved in a long discussion. We were near the completion of the required first-year foundation course, and it was time to declare our majors. I told her I was going to major in painting, as I had planned since first applying to the school. She said she had decided on commercial art. I was reluctant to put her off altogether, but I approached rabidness in my negative assessment of her choice.

She replied, "People have to make a living. You can't make a living by doing paintings. I'll get a job in commercial art and do my own work on weekends." I had often heard this said in the form of advice, as has anyone who expresses an inclination to go to art school.

"If you go that route you will never do your own painting," I countered. Unruly painter and cautious artist, attracted to each other but with a touch of antagonism, we entered a gentle duel of thoughts and eyes. As we exchanged our visions of the lives we would live, I saw her as entangled in all that I had rejected or was still fighting against. We talked for some time, venturing into the deeper waters of economy and philosophy, waters I was sad that I could not see as being bridgeable.

The Ark

On the first night of my second year at art school, in a new lodging on a different street in the Back Bay, I awoke with a start, hearing noises. Someone was moving around or moving something around, and through the cloth drape that was the door to my room I could see a light. No light had been on when I went to bed. There were no neighbors on this floor nor in the rooms above me . . . I should have been completely alone in this part of the building. I lay still and listened. A silent moment, then more rustling about, as though someone was shifting boxes. I rose quietly from my cot and took up a hammer I had left lying on a small bureau near the card table that served as desk, drawing board, and dinner table. I had been using the hammer for some interior decorating, hanging my drapery door and securing the orange-crate bookshelves. Silently I moved to where I could pull aside the drape a sliver and look into the dim light of the outer room.

I saw a sudden shadowy movement, then another, and made out a furtive but unmistakable shape as it passed through a beam of light into darkness. Rats! . . . two rats . . . half a dozen rats; within a minute I counted a dozen. I had never seen them so close up and was surprised by the size and quickness of these representatives of urban wildlife. They were dimly revealed by the streetlight that shone through the small high window whose bottom sash was flush with the sidewalk at the back of the building.

Much relieved that the light was only a streetlight and that the scufflings were caused by nothing worse than rats, I watched my long-tailed neighbors scurry about. Clearly I would have to resign myself to sharing the cellar with them. I couldn't envision any extermination program that would be effective in this building. I slipped my hammer under my pillow and went back to bed.

That first night in my new home would have been the last for many people. Being awakened by the rats' midnight ball did take some of the glow off the high spirits lingering from my first dinnertime in this new place, a rent-free lodging that would go a long way toward helping me survive financially in my second year at the Museum School. I had decided to enter the degree program offered in affiliation with Tufts University, to which students could apply after completing the mandatory first-year foundation program. Originally, envisioning myself as strictly a painter, I had no intention of doing this; but I changed my mind, applied to the bachelor of fine arts program, and was accepted. This decision raised my tuition, added a year to my schooling, and required me to attend classes five and a half days a week.

Students in the same circumstances had scattered all around Boston in search of cheap rooms, lofts, anyplace they could get by. Some banded together in communal quarters, but I preferred to live alone. Visits to dormitories and fraternity houses at other colleges had made me grateful that the Museum School had no student housing.

On a visit with my friend Herb while I was house-hunting, I mentioned that I couldn't afford the ten-dollar-a-week room in the rooming house where I had lived during my first year. I had met Herb through a letter he had written to me regarding an article I had published in the *Philadelphia Herpetological Society Bulletin* on feeding hatchling turtles. I responded, and we became close friends through the mail, though he was sixteen years older than I. He lived in Boston, where I first met him in person when I submitted my portfolio to the Museum School. When I moved into the Back Bay five months later I had a friend-in-residence a couple of blocks away.

Herb was managing a pet shop called the Ark. He told me there was a makeshift room in the cellar under the shop that could be made livable. There would be no need to let anyone know that a two-legged animal was living under the pet shop, and I wouldn't have to pay rent. I could earn my shelter by cleaning cages.

Cheered by this prospect, I met him at the Ark. There were no puppies or kittens in this pet parade; the store was alive with animals more suited to a jungle: agile coatimundis, constantly climbing all over their tree limbs; ear-splitting macaws; a silent, gracefully pacing ocelot; a shadowy, similarly prowling jaguarundi. A nearly invisible anaconda, small at a mere four feet, was coiled beneath his climbing tree among water plants in a pool that could barely contain him. There were turtles and tortoises from all over the world, beautiful, exotic, and saddening to see. A hulk of a spider monkey sat on his swing, carefully looking me over. Did he suspect he had a new roommate?

After introducing me to the denizens of the Ark, Herb opened a door at the back of the shop and escorted me down a shaky set of stairs. I was being shown to my room, the proverbial hole in the wall. Actually it wasn't so much proverbial as literal. A doorless opening in the studs and sheetrock, twenty-nine inches wide, led into an alcove—yes, one could call it an alcove—off the large open space of the cellar. There was no way of telling to what end the trapezoidal space had been framed in. It contained an upright piano, but at nine by thirteen by twelve by nine feet the chamber clearly was not intended to be a concert hall. The piano was there to stay, unless another section of wall was opened up. My musical talents limited me to being an eclectic, appreciative listener; I used the piano as a bookcase. It rounded out my orange-crate library rather nicely.

Notebooks, art supplies, hot plate, record player, gooseneck desk lamps; along with my three chairs, table, cot, and bureau, these set me up for another school year in Boston. Though I was far removed from any Walden Pond, this place brought me intimations of Thoreau's cabin. I had found shelter and an economy I felt could sustain me as I pursued my studies and my own art and writing. I had freedom and solitude, was within reach of society whenever I sought it, and was not without brute neighbors. The monkeys and macaws didn't always finish their fruit and vegetables, bought in bulk at the outdoor markets in Haymarket Square. Herb, whose paycheck was meager and wasn't always there on Friday night, grazed at the shop, as I did. Monkey chow seemed to offer excellent nutrition, but we couldn't get past its dryness and strawlike flavor. The birds' egg biscuit was a special treat.

One task I approached very gingerly was that of cleaning the cage of Cyrus, the spider monkey. This job made me edgier than helping Rosie, the nine-foot, fifty-pound boa constrictor, shed her skin. Before being brought to the Ark by a man who didn't want her anymore, Rosie clearly had been mistreated, and she had a mean disposition, which is rare in boas. Cyrus, named for his resemblance to a dealer who sold animals to the Ark, was big and moody. When I needed to clean his walk-in cage I would toss a banana into a far corner; he would sit down and peel and eat it, watching me attend to his housekeeping.

One morning as I swept his floor, I was jolted by his sudden, forceful landing on my back. He wrapped his arms around my neck in an instantaneous embrace, clasped me with his feet, and wound his long prehensile tail around my waist. I turned slowly to look into his face, directly over my right shoulder. He put his face up to mine, opened his mouth wide, curled back his thick lips, and bared his teeth, which featured canines that looked more appropriate for a wolf than a banana-eater.

"Get down, Cyrus," I said calmly, "get down now." Very slowly I reached back, placed my hands on his coarse-haired thighs, and gently tried to ease him off. His head snapped even closer; he hissed and bared his teeth, tightening his arms around my neck and constricting his tail powerfully enough to affect my breathing. I could feel his remarkable total body strength. Obviously I would not be able to dislodge him by force, and it didn't seem wise to perturb an animal with such a formidable array of teeth inches from my face and neck.

I stood still for some minutes. He relaxed his grip a little but gave no sign of intending to dismount. I had, all too literally, a monkey on my back. I didn't want him to run loose in the shop, but I had to do something. Making every move as nonthreatening as possible, I eased my way out of the cage, walked to the back room, and picked up another banana. My piggyback rider held firm as I returned to the door of his cage. I tossed the banana to the far corner. He immediately leaped from my back, scrambled over to his treat, and calmly began unwrapping it. I closed and bolted his door.

Later in the year horrible howling cries awoke me just before daylight. I had never heard anything so alien and bloodcurdling, like the sounds of an animal screaming in the face of death. Had the ocelot or jaguarundi gotten out of one cage and into another? I took up my hammer and ascended the stairs, moving aside a little tower of cans I kept against my side of the door to clatter down the stairs and sound a wake-up call should some person or animal push the door open in the night. I pulled the door ajar to see Cyrus sitting on the floor of his cage, hitting his chest and screaming. Who knows what turn of the year in another hemisphere, what message from the natural history that yet lived within him, inspired this wild shrieking at dawn in a city far from his native rain forest.

Drawing, Painting, Writing

I foundered in my first year of drawing and design, which I had expected to be my strengths. I did not disagree that the discipline was important, but I could not spark to drawing bone-white spheres, cubes, pyramids, and such. No Platonic draftsman, I was not at home in the world of pure forms. I struggled with straight lines and geometric proportion and could not draw a proper ellipse to save my life. My skills were better adapted to natural forms and the landscape.

In spring I had my first real breakthrough in drawing class when we spent a week at the Franklin Park Zoo. The long sessions of observing and drawing the zoo animals proved inspirational. I was moved by the mystery and majesty of these wild ones hopelessly removed from their rightful places. I identified with these animals I drew, who would live out their lives in a zoo, as I did with my fellow creatures aboard the Ark. But I had a far longer leash than they did, and a reasonable dream of finding my way back to a landscape suited to my nature.

I saw the patterns in their movements as well as in their fur and feathers. Lions and polar bears would pace rhythmically for a

Zoo sketches.

minute or two or sometimes longer, then come to a standstill in their constrained roaming. Where were they traveling in their minds? Sometimes they kept all four feet in place and rocked back and forth or swayed from side to side for some minutes; at other times they simply lay still. I roughed out sketches while they were on the move or stationary. Then I worked these into more complete drawings, picking up the appropriate sheet of paper when a subject returned to one of the poses I had in progress.

Later Herb got a job at the Franklin Park Zoo. After hours I would follow him on his keeper's rounds and join him in closer contact with some of his charges, even wrestling with lion cubs. These kittens, nearly my size, bowled me over, cuffed me off balance, slipped by me with supple silence, restrained power, and consummate grace. I gained a most tangible appreciation for a life form far different from anything I had ever taken in hand in my native swamps. The zoo gave me my first commission, a series of paintings of animals for signs on their cages, for which I was paid ten dollars each.

My own nature and my immersion in nature, as well as my innate sense of design, line, and composition, led me to gravitate more toward Eastern than Western art. I was especially drawn to Japanese screen paintings and Chinese scrolls. Nature itself was a theme in these works rather than a mere background for human life and history, as seemed to be the case in most Western painting. Ocean waves and rocks were subjects enough for profound visual expression, as were cranes, carp, and turtles; bamboo, pine, and plum trees (the "three gentlemen" of Chinese painting); wind and water—all had life and meaning even when no human figure appeared in the work. *Rabbits and Crows in the Night Snow, Birds and a Marshy Stream,* or *River Landscape with Fireflies*—the subjects indicated by these poetic titles were as valued as those of any great battle or religious scene. I was struck by the use of space in Asian art, the void as counterpoint to image, and the union of decorative, naturalistic, and abstract qualities in a single painting.

But I was also attracted to certain aspects of Western art. I became deeply absorbed in the egg tempera panels of pre-Renaissance Italy and the paintings of Botticelli, as well as medieval illuminated manuscripts and Dürer's studies of plants and animals. I learned to work in egg tempera, to grind my own pigments, mix them with water, and dip the mixture into the yolk of an egg, brushful by brushful, painting on panels I prepared with gesso and polished with agate. I did a copy of a detail from Botticelli's *Birth of Venus*, then another from an original work in the museum archives, an anonymous early Sienese panel painting of a bearded saint writing in a book. In this second copy I laid and tooled gold leaf. The materials captivated me as much as the methods. Ultramarine, alizarin crimson, umbers, ochers, siennas—the pigments glowed with brilliance or deep richness from the dark interiors of their paper bags, earths so rare they seemed unearthly. The sharp white of gesso, made from whiting and rabbit-skin glue, the gleam of its agate-polished surface on a poplar panel, and the way it took the stroke-by-stroke trailings of pigment and egg yolk from fine-pointed sable brushes made painting seem like magic as well as art. Sheets of gold leaf, transparent when held in the air, became solid gold when laid on red clay bole applied over gesso. I worked with powdered jewels and sheets of gold, rendering folds in cloth, the semitransparent skin of Venus, the fine white hairs of the bearded saint.

I believed in my heart of hearts that even if I could not have been in the first rank of artists of that brilliant pre–oil painting era, I at least could have found a place in the studio of Simone Martini or another Sienese master, or in Botticelli's workshop. And even though I was not of the culture and had been raised with pencils and pens in my hand rather than brushes, I felt I could have found work with the great Japanese screen painters of the Kano school, or with masters like Hasegawa Tohaku, Kaiho Yusho, or Ogata Korin. I had missed such opportunities only by half a millennium and half a world or so.

Even as I explored the techniques of early panel painting, I was also becoming increasingly immersed in the art of the early twentieth century. I was inspired immediately by the work of Paul Klee and the German Expressionists, then more gradually by Picasso and by Miró and Kandinsky to some extent, I was drawn to the Cubist work of Picasso and Gris, and to the surrealist and metaphysical painters, principally de Chirico and Magritte.

During my time in the urban art-and-ideas world of studios, museums, books, and fellow artists, nature tended to come more from within myself. I entered an extended and necessary field

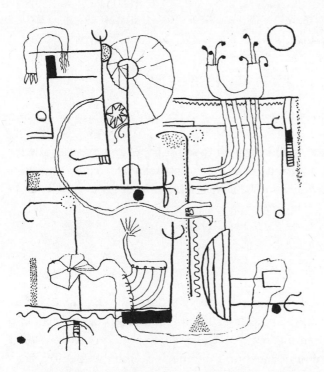

I suppose
It had something
To do with the sea
And the strange things
Always in it
And the way the moon
Pushed up one tide
While drawing another
Off the land
And the fact
That the sun
Has burnt itself out
In the sea
Every night
For numberless years.

A page from my handbound Book of a Number of Hours.

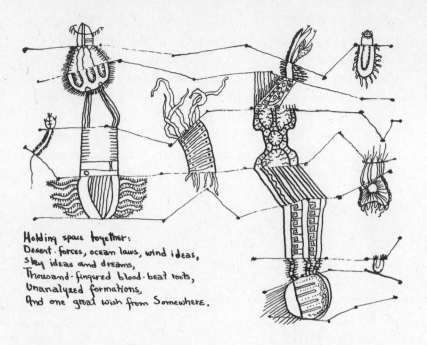

Holding space together:
Desert-forces, ocean laws, wind ideas,
sky ideas and dreams,
Thousand-fingered blood-beat roots,
Unanalyzed formations,
And one great wish from Somewhere.

A page from Book of a Number of Hours.

season of the self, withdrawing into mindscapes and dream gardens of mingled memory and imagination, constellations of the heart, interior places of desire and belief, the landscape of my own heart and mind.

Laurette

On the first day of the final semester of my second year, I observed a new classmate in the painting studio. Little Miss Commercial Art had become a painting major. We had not come in contact since our locker-room summit meeting of some nine months before. The class was working on large paintings, four by eight feet or so, and we had to construct our own stretchers, stretch raw canvas on them, and prime them with gesso before painting with oils. Though inept at any form of carpentry, I had somehow mastered this process, and I offered her my assistance. With my guidance her first canvas came out beautifully. To show her gratitude she took me out for pie and coffee. The short version, when I later told of our getting together, that Laurette fed me and I never went home, was not terribly far from the truth.

Our background was the painting studio, with its sea of canvases, heavy scents of oil paint, turpentine, and damar varnish, and the coming of spring along the Muddy River. We began to hang out together, walking and talking in the Fens. I started to make dangerous sense to her.

Laurette told me that when she had first met me she thought I was something of a wild man and that I thought upside-down. I told her that actually I thought backward. One of my secrets of survival since beginning to understand the spoken word was to run everything I was told the other way around. That way it made sense; I would always find an answer, if not the whole truth. On an evening walk as spring was deepening, she said to me, "At last I know someone who can express the things I think and feel."

"Every time I see you, someone is telling you her troubles," she said. Laurette was engaged, complete with diamond ring. As her engagement was a troubled one I saw her in times of happiness and times of sorrow. We went for coffee one morning in early May, a mutual acquaintance joining us. A silent communication ran beneath the conversation as Laurette pointed to the ring finger of her left hand, no longer sparkling with a diamond.

When Laurette first visited me, I was living in the cellar under the pet shop, sleeping with a hammer under my pillow. On the thin edge both emotionally and physically, I weighed 139 pounds and had ten dollars in my bank, a Japanese green-tea tin. Little more than a month later, as we sat in the Fens, I said, "I think someday I'd like to have you for my wife."

"Someday I would like to be your wife," she said.

Queensbury Street

In early April of that year the Ark was foundering; it was inevitable that it would go out of business. Then the owner of the building hanged himself in the subcellar beneath my room. The building was sold, and Herb, the animals, and I were dispersed. Only the free-range rats remained, but they too were evicted when the building was razed to make way for the War Memorial Auditorium. The ink-and-brush murals I had done on my sheetrock walls of "Manimals," Minotaur-like figures, part man and part animal, were lost.

I found a room for twenty-five dollars a month on Columbus Avenue in a building where some other painting students were fixing up a studio loft. It came with a communal bathroom in which there was a shared refrigerator. When it was time to move, I piled my cot high with a collapsible writing table, blankets, art supplies, and books and pushed my squeaky-wheeled moving van along Boylston Street in the night.

By the time Laurette and I became a pair, I had moved up in the world—to the third floor at least. I'm not sure my radiator ever got warm to the touch, but it was warmer inside the building than outside. And besides, it was spring and I was in love.

In mid-June there came a hard parting, as Laurette went back to her native Portsmouth, New Hampshire, to work and I returned to Connecticut to try to earn enough money for another school year. Separation did not work, and we exchanged visits throughout the summer. She had not experienced the natural world but knew of my love for it, so she took me over a narrow bridge to a wooded island with bouldered shores, as though leading a captive wildling to a place where it could be at home. I took her to Cedar Pastures, to hidden corners where I could show her vestiges of what I had known. And I took her to the Millers' house, set in a patch of lingering woods in a region almost entirely converted to roads and houses. Laurette's bonding with Bill and DeDe was immediate and deep.

In September I returned to Boston determined not to live as close to the edge as I had for the previous two years; I didn't want to continue that way, and I didn't want Laurette to have to. When I returned for my third year still owing money for the second, the school secretary told me she had written "Will pay when he can, leave him alone" on my file. A financial aid officer at Tufts helped me get a college loan and unearthed an obscure scholarship reserved for redheads who showed promise. After looking over my financial aid form, he told me he did not believe that anyone could live in Boston and go to school for two years on so little money.

Laurette and I found a basement apartment on Queensbury Street, just across the Fens from the museum. It wasn't exactly legal, but it had five rooms and cost half as much as any other rental we had looked at.

Laurette worked at the museum bookstore; I worked part-time as a museum guard. Uniformed, shiny-badged, armed with a police whistle and a flashlight, I filled in for vacationing regulars. I sought assignments in the Asian galleries among the Chinese scrolls and Japanese screens. I became all the more immersed. These works, from a great carp in weedy water to bare willows and distant mountains, to highly abstracted waves, clouds, and dragons, struck me more and more as ultimate evocations of nature and landscape, human emotions and philosophy. Ink-and-brush washes on silk dissolved barriers between nature and man, the real and the abstract, painting and writing.

Even though I was the one with the badge, I felt like a prisoner. The painting studios just across the street were closed for the summer. I could look out windows in one direction and see the Fens. I took to doing pocket-size drawings from imagination—abstract configurations of arabesque lines, areas of crosshatching and stippling, compositions in pen and colored inks featuring forms suggestive of seashells, plants, turtle shells, and other subjects from nature. Sometimes I incorporated lines of invented script into these "organic abstracts." The size of the drawings was dictated by the need to stuff a work in progress into my pocket should the lieutenant or, worse yet, the captain of the guard force steal upon me and find my attention straying from my charge. I wondered if there had ever been a museum guard whose work ended up in the museum he once guarded.

As I paced my favorite galleries, my mind would roam to remembered landscapes. How differently these same hours were going in marshes along the railroad tracks and tidal creek, the fields and thickets of Cedar Pastures—even, just beyond the museum walls, in the heavily compromised environment of the Fens. In a swamp or marsh, along a stream, the seasons moved forward through time and ended, while appearing to return to the same points year after year. Every turtle sighting was new, even of the same turtle on the same emerald-mossed blueberry island. My mind and spirit journeyed with the slow spinning of a day through the landscape of earth, the landscape of time. As a museum guard I came to a keener understanding of the difference between indoor time and outdoor time, how little indoor time had to do with light, a moment in a season, or a place in the universe.

After our son, Sean, was born in August, following my third year at the Museum School, Laurette put aside her painting for a time and devoted herself to being a full-time mother. I scrambled on, working at my various jobs and finishing my school courses, but I still found time to go looking for turtles in the Fens.

In making my rounds of the reedier places one summer afternoon, I heard thrashings in the water. It sounded like people swimming; but this could not be, not in the Muddy River, at least not voluntarily. The commotion I heard seemed greater than any splashings the largest carp could generate. I stalked through giant reeds and ankle-deep shallows to where I could see a narrow open inlet. As I looked in, sudden surges churned the water. Carp. It was carp, after all, and they were muddying the muddy river all the more. I could barely make out the big fish, though they roiled partway out of the water at times. I wondered if they were spawning. Then, several yards out, something else broke the surface.

The flattened dome of a tremendous carapace—a muddy, mossy, green-tinged brown—cruised slowly, deliberately, paralleling the shoreline a few yards out from the ructious fish. A snapping turtle, as big as any I had ever seen, was on the prowl. I watched the great shield slide along, then turn in a gradual arc toward the shallows. Carp surged wildly as the turtle turned. I wondered how they could see anything in the water, how they could sense the whereabouts of the one stalking them, who could become an even more awesome living mystery of the Muddy River simply by submerging, a massive, invisible prowling presence. The turtle too, must have been using senses other than sight as he tracked his quarry. Some kind of sonar, some reading of underwater pulses, must have been guiding both predator and prey. Eyes would be of service only at deadliest close range. I never saw a snapping turtle's shell that looked more like an armored tank, like a plated submarine.

The turtle seemed to be herding the unnerved carp, driving them into the shallows. I could not fathom why the menaced fish did not turn tail and bolt to broader, deeper water. During the quarter of an hour or so that I stood watching, the turtle did not raise his head. When the shell advanced after a pause or shifted directions, a great swirling of water came up as the fish changed places. No one wanted to be "it" in this game of tag. Evidently the carp managed to stay just out of range; I never saw the snapping turtle make a strike.

The following day the gargantuan turtle was at the same place. I watched and waited until he cruised as close to shore as I thought he was likely to come, then I stepped into the water—and sank knee-deep in mud. The shell held still, then began to glide away. I made a grab at the saw-toothed back end of the great carapace. The spiked tail and the hind legs with their sharp-clawed feet came to life, as did the sluggish river—water and mud churning, fish, turtle, and man thrashing and splashing. It was a long, hard struggle—the mud was my adversary as much as the turtle—but at last I beached the powerful animal, and after several loud, snapping-jawed strikes he settled down. We were both a little worn out from our bout of mud wrestling.

I had had dreams about wrestling with snapping turtles and with snakes, which were always much bigger than they are in reality. I never felt fearful. These were not nightmares exactly, just sustained grapplings with impressive animals I had had such tangible relationships with since boyhood. The feelings were so precise: the scales of the snake, the muscles beneath the skin, the writhing strength as coils wrapped and unwrapped around my arms and body and I worked constantly to keep a grip just behind the head, keep the open mouth and recurved teeth away from me. The snapping turtles in my dreams had muscular, surprisingly agile legs and feet, a heavily spiked tail that seemed like a fifth leg, extraordinarily powerful serpentlike neck and head, a wide-open mouth with shearing jaws. I awoke from these dreams exhausted.

Now I rested my hand on the turtle's muddy shell, wondering at his age and history. I looked into his eyes, with their starburst pattern and the fixed stare that imparted an extreme distance, set in a massive head. What was Boston like when, as a hatchling, he first dug out of his nest and made his way to the Muddy River? I had a feeling there were no cars on the surrounding roadways and that the paint was not yet dry on some of the canvases that were to end up in the heralded Impressionist collection of the Fine Arts Museum.

I did not want to trouble this exceptional turtle any more, but I could not resist trying to take him home to be weighed and photographed. I moved him to open ground but couldn't very well carry him, even for a short distance, let alone all the way to my apartment. As I sat pondering what to do, a small crowd began to assemble, mostly gardeners from the Victory Gardens. One of my fellow painters happened along and agreed to help. I slid a board beneath the turtle and we managed to lift him, I holding the base of his tail like a rudder. After a brief flurry of protest the turtle had settled into calm resignation and seemed agreeable to, or at least tolerant of, going along for the ride.

As two policemen approached, I had a dread that they might be inclined to dispatch the beast and save the city from the Creature from the Muddy River. But they were most cooperative when I told them I was from the Museum of Science and that I was taking the turtle for documentation and would be releasing it soon, just where

I had caught it. They even helped hold back the growing assemblage, including a woman who kept trying to poke the turtle with her hoe. Another painter friend came along, the only one in the studio who owned a car. As we drove away with the turtle in the back of his station wagon, I saw an SPCA truck pull up, yellow lights flashing.

When I came home bearing the lord of the Muddy River, Laurette's deep acceptance, even encouragement, of my devotion to turtles wavered some. I got a big carton from a grocer and weighed it empty and then with the turtle hunkered down inside it: forty-six pounds. We had a big, old-fashioned bathtub, and when he stretched out in it full length, the snapping turtle reached from one end to the other, nose tip to tail tip, four and a half feet.

The next afternoon, while I was at school, Laurette looked down the hall to see the turtle teetering on the edge of the bathtub, about to drop to the floor. She grabbed our infant son and fled the apartment. Just outside the door she encountered my brother John, who was staying in Boston for a time, and relayed her tale of terror. Taking up a long-handled dust mop, John strode into the bathroom and nudged the turtle back into the tub with a fluffy thrust. When I got home I assured Laurette that I had never met a turtle who could turn a doorknob; all she needed to do was to close the bathroom door. And we would not have lost our only child in any case; snapping turtles can't eat when they are out of the water.

We needed our tub back and the turtle needed to return to the comforting turbidity of the Muddy River. The next morning, in a driving rain, which I assumed would keep an audience from gathering, I had a friend drop me and the turtle off at the Victory Gardens. The turtle was quite placable by now, and I could carry him, with pauses to rest, by taking handholds at the front and back of his carapace. With admiration and gratitude, I watched that great turtle high-step among the reeds and submerge in the muddy waters of his home.

Farewell to Cedar Pastures

During my final year at art school, on a holiday visit to Connecticut, I went to Cedar Pastures. I rolled on the ground in the bleached winter grass, ran my hands over apple bark, brushed among the cedars, and rubbed myself with sprigs of bayberry and sweetfern. I circled the ice-rimmed black water of the turtle pondings. Gulls cried out above the cove. A flock of bluebirds in black cherry and sumac along the wall and furtive assemblages of sparrows and other small birds in greenbrier thickets were my only company. In late December's early dusk I watched the sun set through sienna and smoke-gray mazes of highbush blueberry, swamp azalea, sweet pepperbush, and scarlet-fruited winterberry: a thin blaze of crimson low in the west, flared with gold, set in sunlight-edged purple-black gatherings of cloud.

Color burned out of the sky, but light lingered in the bronzy glow of little bluestem and switchgrass. In the cold, wintry silence the red cedars looked more than ever like druid trees. Streetlamps and house lights came on to the east, where newly built houses had replaced oaks and hickories on the ridge.

Cedar Pastures had been up for sale, and it seemed certain that this turtle island would be swallowed up by the surrounding sea of industry, commerce, and suburbia. But a campaign to save it as open space had led to a last-minute deal in which the old farmland was purchased by the state. I understood that this was meant to be good news. Many people rejoiced, but I knew the place was lost; it was being saved by being sacrificed.

After stateparkhood had been in place for a couple of years, I went back to walk the lowland trail, early on a bone-chilling, rainy midweek morning in March. The hour and the weather offered the best hope for a measure of solitude. I found signs, fences, pathways—at least motorized vehicles were excluded. A boulevard-like entranceway linked up with the lowland trail. For the first fifty yards or more past the entrance, the broad, graveled jogging and cycling path was lined on both sides by dog crap. A well-beaten path led from the cinder track to the boulder-lined pool where I had first seen a spotted turtle in this fallow farmland. Cigarette butts floated alongside some wood-frog eggs. The main recreational artery passed close to the chain of pools I had known so well. In those days they had been hidden, secrets of the turtles' landscape; now nearly all of them had well-trampled byways leading to them. But clutches of eggs indicated that wood frogs and spotted salamanders were still present. And spotted turtles could be holding out in the heavily thicketed margins of the permanent pond, where thorny tangles and treacherous muck shielded their last bastion of hiding places.

The chill morning advanced. I stepped back among the alders as a track team ran by. I heard shouts and the slamming of car doors: the hour of arrival. As I walked the last bit of the lowland trail, a couple jogged in, he with three leashed dogs, she with two. Then more running feet, spinning mountain-bike wheels, dogs on the loose. The place had not been clearcut, paved, and lawned at least. No doubt it was billed as a wildlife sanctuary. But it had become one more playground, another human theme park, an ecological and spiritual graveyard in the making.

MIDDLE YEARS

Druid. Take, if you must, this little bag of dreams;
   Unloose the cord, and they will wrap you round.

—William Butler Yeats, "Fergus and the Druid"

Big Sandy Pond

THE INTIMATE Museum School graduation ceremony was held, sans caps and gowns, sans pomp and circumstance, in the garden courtyard of the Museum of Fine Arts. Some champagne and sandwiches, a few brief words, goodbyes with a finality that was somehow not anticipated, and a small band of painters was more out in the world now that they were out of art school. Studios would be diverse and difficult to come by. Perhaps finding, or even recognizing, the next studio would be the hardest part.

An opening came up for me at the museum bookstore, and I transferred out of the guard force. Laurette and I were expecting our second child in October. There was no going back to where either of us had come from when we arrived at art school five years before. We needed to find a new place; I needed to find a landscape with turtles. Although showing up in homeroom five mornings a week was not my goal when I set off for art school and not my first choice upon graduating, our best option seemed to be for me to teach high school art. Listings of job openings were sparse, and my quest was not aided by the fact that I had opted for the BFA program instead of pursuing a bachelor of science in education degree. This meant that I had not done any practice teaching and had not been certified to teach in public schools. I sent my resumé here and there, and well into summer, with time running out, I finally got an interview.

I boarded a bus bound for Silver Lake Regional High School in Kingston, only thirty-five miles away from Boston. As I rode south, the urban landscape gave way to nothing more promising than horizons of rooftops in the immediately surrounding towns, followed by a panorama of slightly more separated roofs, driveways, and small yards, many of which had been converted to swimming pools. The markedly unvarying, unimaginative pattern of the human patchwork quilt being imposed on the landscape of my turtle-and-swamp boyhood had here been filled in completely decades ago. Farther out, the dwellings, lawns, and roads were more widely separated. Scatterings of fields and woods began to appear.

I got off the bus at a general store in what looked like a hopefully small town and set off on the two-and-a-half-mile walk to the high school. Route 27 was a blessedly light-traveled highway. I decided not to make a first impression as a hitchhiker in the town in which I was seeking a position as a public school teacher. For the first time in years I walked along a roadway that was lined not with buildings but with pine woods and old fields. White pine and quaking aspen took the place of red cedar and black cherry in advancing upon abandoned hayfields here.

About halfway to my destination I saw that the road was too heavily traveled for some. Crushed and flattened, the ornately patterned shell of a road-killed box turtle stopped me in my tracks. I stared at it for a long time, then scanned the surrounding sandy fields and pine woods. How much time did I have? Not enough to look for turtles . . . couldn't be late for my first, and quite possibly only, teaching interview. But I was certain that if I did end up in this town, I would find box turtles. They had not been part of my turtle world in Connecticut; my only experience with this species came from my two visits to Gordon's grandparents' place on Long Island. At that time, box turtles and their habitats were disappearing there even more quickly than spotted turtles from Connecticut.

Here was a sign, if a sad one, in orange-tinged creamy yellow hieroglyphs on an amber and mahogany ground; the eloquent script of the turtle's life pattern had not yet faded from tortoiseshell-like scutes just beginning to exfoliate from tablets of white bone.

With better fortune the annihilated dome could have housed a turtle life of a century's duration. I licked my fingertips and rubbed them over a loose carapace scute. Moistened, the turtle's arabesque signature came to life for a moment. Slipping this talisman into my pocket, I continued my journey.

I had no other teaching interviews, but I had the great good fortune of not needing another. Three weeks later the call came from Silver Lake—I had given the school the phone number of the museum sales desk—telling me they wanted me to be the high school art teacher.

I walked across the Fens wondering how I would break the epochal news to Laurette. She was hanging velour drapes when I came in, a prize find from the Goodwill store earlier that afternoon.

"Do you think they'll like the drapes in Kingston?" I asked. As she was always quite single-minded when working on a painting or putting a newfound thrift-shop treasure into service, the question didn't register. She began telling me the details of this latest acquisition, most enhancing to our artistic Queensbury Street abode.

"Do you think they'll like the drapes in Kingston?" I repeated. This time my meaning sunk in.

⸎

In Pembroke, one of the four towns in the school district, we rented a little cedar-shingled cottage on a small reservoir called Big Sandy Pond. The porch was right above the shore; at full flood the water would be no more than a few paces from the steps. The cottage, squeezed between the pond and a road, had a yard not much bigger than our basement apartment. A neighboring cottage stood close by on one side, but the shoreline in the other direction was uninhabited, a narrow riparian band of trees and shrubs. Given the setting, we could overlook the cottage's bright turquoise exterior. The canary yellow, robin's egg blue, and magenta interiors could be repainted with something more in harmony with our paintings, drawings, and prints—and the dark green velour drapes.

We could not afford to have the gas and phone hooked up, but then we had never had a phone in Boston. We could manage without a refrigerator for a while and wouldn't be needing heat for weeks. The electricity was on, so we had lights and could use our electric coffeepot, electric frying pan, and toaster. For transportation I had an English bike borrowed from a friend. The little art family settled in: Laurette, Sean, and I, new one due in six weeks or so, and a lingering collection of turtle refugees from my time at the Ark.

Around twilight of our first day, as I was putting the last turtles and books in place, I discovered in the kitchen cabinets two hand lines with their familiar green cord, hooks, and sinkers. The great pond surely held bullheads. After dark I descended the little planked stairway to the broad sandy shore. Without a refrigerator we couldn't keep much perishable food on hand, but I had bought a package of hot dogs for supper and set the leftovers on a cool pond-side window ledge. I baited hooks with hot dog rings and threw two lines as far out as I could, among stars reflected on still black water.

Just the previous evening I had been sitting on the warm stonework outside our basement apartment in the never-really-dark of the city nocturne, drinking wine coolers in heat that brick and blacktop had collected during the glaring hot August day and were radiating back to the night. Sounds of people and muted music drifted out from open windows, bits of conversation floated down from passersby on the sidewalk. Now I was on sand still warm from the day, in the gathering night coolness of the pond depression, with no sounds except the cadence of crickets, no light but the stars in the deep black sky and their reflections on the unwavering black plane of the pond.

Lake-stars rode the concentric ripples emanating from the heavy fall of my two sinkers. The gentle undulations settled out, and constellations I had not viewed in five years were mirrored before me, as fixed on the water as in the sky above. Had I forgotten these seemingly unwheeling turnings?

Tug, tug . . . Although I had not fished for bullheads since I was twelve years old, the signal from the bottom-feeding fish was unmistakable. I restrained myself and let my quarry take the bait. With a sharp pull from my end I had a fish on the line. I could tell at once that this was a far bigger bullhead than any I had caught in boyhood. There was a decidedly weighty, bulldog resistance to my hand-over-handing the taut line to shore. Creaking and thrashing, the heavy black fish hit the pale sand beach.

Not wishing to deal with the sturdy, sharp-barbed fins of this rambunctious bullhead in the dark, I ran up to the house with him still struggling on hook and line. I measured the fish at sixteen inches before beheading and cleaning him. The prospect of eating this favorite fish, which I had not tasted in so many years, gave me appetite enough for a second supper. Laurette cooked him up on the spot, though it troubled her that the fish's mouth, on a newspaper on the counter, continued to open and close as she was frying up the rest of him. Gingerly she tasted her first bullhead and liked it. Thoreau had had pickerel to augment his frugal economy at Walden

Pond, and we would have bullhead at Big Sandy Pond. Before long I added eel and perch, though the former, so hard to get off the hook and prepare for frying, never became a regular part of our menu.

The next night I went out under the stars to fish again. Scanning the shallows with a flashlight, I made out the shell of a musk turtle, a moving stone among unmoving stones, then his pointed head with its pale

A musk turtle.

yellow pinstriping. In a few more sweeps my beam caught another. I had turtles for neighbors. There were no houses along most of the reservoir's shore, and the weedy backwater embayments surely supported painted and snapping turtles as well as musk turtles. Big Sandy Pond was not as wild as the Old Swamp or Cedar Pastures in their glory days, but it was considerably wilder than the Fens. That night I watched these graceful bottom-walkers prowl among stones for prey—small crayfish, snails, insect larvae, and the like—then tossed out my lines, trusting that there were none of their kin in deeper water to be attracted to the hot dog rings on my hooks.

A neighbor who lived on a hill across the road from us couldn't help but notice that the young family who had moved into the turquoise cottage had no car—and also that the wife, the mother of a two-year-old son, was heavily pregnant. Mary Lydon introduced herself to Laurette and in a not-unfriendly manner asked if her husband was going to take her to the hospital on his bicycle when it came time to have the baby. Laurette explained that she had been a clinic patient at Boston Lying-in during this pregnancy, as she had been with our firstborn, but we weren't sure where we'd be going for the delivery. Mary, who had recently lost her mother, had driven back and forth to Boston in the final stages of her mother's illness and had become used to the trip. Now home all the time, she offered to drive Laurette to Boston Lying-in when the time came, which it did on the sixth of October, when our daughter, Riana Frost, was born.

When Bill and DeDe's daughter Claire was five years old, I had written and illustrated "The Story of Alia" for her. I had made up the name Alia and invented a name for a river in the tale, "the slow-winding River Riana." Upon reading my story, Laurette said that if we ever had a daughter she wanted to name her Riana. "Frost" sounded good with this and honored the poet who was one of our mainstay inspirations at our setting out together. So we had two children, Sean Michael and Riana Frost, before we had our first car.

In our three years on Big Sandy Pond, I taught, did drawings, and took turtle-season time, wading and wandering cranberry bogs, the backwaters of larger ponds, fields, and woods. Laurette was content to put her painting aside and devote most of her time to Sean and Riana and life by the lake. She knew it would be impossible to get involved with a painting, have to tear herself away at frequent intervals to pay attention to the little ones, and then try to get back into the painting. She turned to less all-consuming works, such as hooked rugs, clay vessels, and ceramic figures.

Teaching

When school opened, I rode my bike five miles each way for several days, until I met colleagues who offered me rides. The first few days of teaching I came home exhausted, went to bed, got up for dinner, then went right back to bed. But I eased into the demands and became energized by the agreeable and increasingly creative atmosphere that evolved in my art room. I always had a plan but never a lesson plan. There were too many possibilities; I discovered an inexhaustible idea-mine as I watched my students do their work. I relished the camaraderie that came forth as we all got to know one another. The art room became a place of art, poetry, and humor.

I started the year off by having each of my students make a handbound book in which to blend drawing, painting, collage, and writing, either their own or quotations from favorite sources.

"What are you going to do in your book?" I asked Russell.

"I'm going to write 'Ten of the World's Greatest Mineral Poems.'"

He went on to do just that, and he read his unique poems to an enthusiastically appreciative class. I distributed mimeographed copies to other art classes. Not known as a stellar student in other subjects, Russell became a legend in the art room.

"What next?" I asked him when his mineral opus was completed.

"Ten of the World's Greatest Animal Poems."

He didn't go on to the plant kingdom, but he did pen such

classics as "No, I Shall Never See Spain" and "The Poor Egyptian's Daughter." Russell was not one for drawing or painting in the realistic sense, but when he turned from the literary to the visual side of his imagination he created some remarkable abstract drawings and paintings. It was sometimes difficult to explain to the art room's traditionalists the high grades I gave Russell and other more conceptual artists. Attempting to emulate Russell's success, Tony came up to me with an indigestibly colored splashwork. Uncharacteristically, I was at a loss for words.

Tony broke the silence. "You don't like it, do you, David? I can tell just by the way you threw up."

As Danny put it, "Beauty is only skin deep, but ugly goes all the way to the bone."

Though I was not as laissez-faire as my chief mentor (I knew of no one who could be), the tone of my high school teaching was decidedly Milleresque. I tended to offer suggestions and instruction to individuals on their undertakings of the moment rather than teaching the class as a whole.

"You don't teach too much, do you?" Mr. Miller said when I first visited him after taking to the road he was still traveling.

"No, Bill, I let out a lot of line, let them discover."

We started a magazine, a collection of art, poetry, and prose that was published every couple of months, calling it *Voiceprints* after Jeff reported that each person's voice could be electronically transcribed into markings that were as unique to the individual as his or her fingerprints.

We did a good deal of drawing from nature. In autumn I introduced the work of Paul Klee. We did magic-square watercolors— Klee-like juxtapositions of rectangles that reflected the colors and moods of season—and papered the room with them. We made calendars, which we lettered, numbered, and ornamented like illuminated manuscripts; we carved "spirit sticks" in found pieces of branch or root, then painted and inlaid them with pebbles, shells, or bits of bone; we worked in clay, hand-building goblets and ceramic boxes; we did copies of Old Masters, cut blockprint *ex libris* designs for our personal libraries, and painted landscapes.

More than ever I became convinced that we peak somewhere around age eleven, that adolescence, the high school years, is all too often a final flowering. It seemed to me that the great diminishing, if not extinguishing, of individuality and creativity that comes at the transition to what is

called adulthood has much to do with cherished notions and is driven by societal structures and expectations, a "way-it-has-to-be" that so many of us never voted for. The electric self becomes lost in the beauty, joy, and disaster of job, career, house, car, spouse, and kids, set to the tune of duty and acquisition: the "American Dream."

Turtles

The four towns in the school district were still surprisingly rural, considering that they were only thirty to forty miles south of Boston. That first autumn I was talking turtles with some of my students, asking if they ever saw spotted or box turtles. One of them, Danny, told me he saw spotted turtles on occasion, and in fact had recently seen a couple that were not much bigger than a quarter. These had to be hatchlings recently emerged from the nest.

Following the map my student-friend made for me, I came to a cranberry bog that seemed to be abandoned and reverting to the wild. Blue and white asters loud with bees, goldenrod well attended by a varied host of pollinators, and bronzing tufts of little bluestem stood here and there on marooning mats of cranberry leaves. The geometrically patterned ditchings held six to ten inches of water, channels largely covered by the pads of white and yellow water lilies still in bloom. I thought back to railroad ditches where hatchling spotted turtles basked hidden in swirls of sedge and mats of cattail, and of the cranberry depression at Cedar Pastures, with its rose pogonias and itinerant spotted turtles. In looking for turtles by species, I consider the place, comparing and contrasting it with the store of pictures-to-go-by that has accrued continually since that early June evening of my eighth year. By this, my twenty-third year, my first year of my teaching, some of these places existed only in memory, living on in my bank of search-images.

I scanned the tangles of cranberry vines hanging over the west-facing banks of the ditches. Another plant that had come to speak to me of spotted turtles and that served here as a sign of a return of wildness, bristly dewberry, laced its thorned, glossy-leaved wands and shiny black fruits among scarlet-fruited cranberries. I preferred to call this long-vined, trailing plant by one of its old names: running swamp blackberry. After originally having come to know them as nameless but familiar life-forms, I couldn't seem to have enough names for the animals and plants dearest to me.

My eyes searched intently, seeking the edge of a carapace or fragment of its pattern among fruits and leaves, sun-sparks and shadows, in a color field of maroon, bronzed green, jet-black and crimson weavings, a layering bewildering to the point of brilliant blindness in the low-slanting October sunlight. A visual near-chaos ruled the microhabitat I scanned, scrambled signals overlaid with a confusion of new and familiar arrangements in a setting I seemed to know even though I had never been here before.

The pure love of—and need for—searching came back to me, a way of seeing reawakened. My eyes roved a minute landscape that on the one hand my mind was simply delighted to take in and on the other was anxious to interpret. Seeing was physical and metaphysical—direct, intuitive, and investigational—as though one eye was that of an artist, the other the eye of a naturalist. In tandem they turned back in time to become the searching eyes of an eight-year-old boy out looking for turtles.

Remembering and envisioning hatchling spotted turtles, I searched the borders of the bog off open sandy terrain, a place of sweetfern that suggested turtle nesting. In a blur of past and present, drifting into the now, I endeavored to shift into turtle time, the time within time that is neither past nor present but the ongoing now.

I watched a water snake unwind and disappear in viny water. I had seen a toad on sand, in sweetfern shade, and glimpsed a smooth green snake gliding into aster shadows at the brushy border of the bog. Ribbon snakes threaded among cranberry vines in the shallowest depressions, and I caught a little redbelly snake. The scarlet belly scales it was loath to display rivaled the brilliance of the fully ripe cranberries. Golden-throated bullfrog and bronze-eyed green frog, the umber-squared back of a pickerel frog . . . it was as though the entire bestiary of my boyhood was being given back to me on this early autumn afternoon. Looking over the bog that so many plants and animals appeared to be reclaiming, I thought, "If a place is left alone it will come back; it will all come back."

And then a dusty, coal-black bit of shell, the curve of a tiny carapace caught my eye—not the form-revealing outline of an entire shell, only a section of the rounded rim in sun-penetrated cover. The crowning of the bestiary . . . I took up the sun-warmed hatchling spotted turtle, his shallow-domed carapace bearing thirteen pale

Hatchling spotted turtles.

yellow suns, one on each of the five vertebral scutes and the pleurals bordering them, four on each side. Several of his marginals and his head bore tinier suns, some yellow, some orange. Remembering well my first shaking hold on a turtle, my hand shook a bit as I held this gift of the cranberry bog in the palm of my hand.

I found two more hatchlings, each of them tucked among vines, tilted toward the sun, all three perfectly placed in their world, the way it always is with turtles. It seemed that I needed only to find the right place in the landscape and be there, and I would be given turtles. As I set the nascent turtles back in place, my mind slipped away from the entrancing season of the moment and I thought of the spotted turtles I would surely find here in the spring.

On one of my last visits to the cranberry bog that fall, the owner

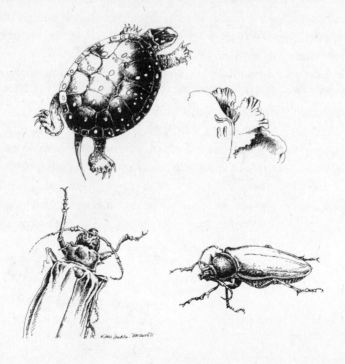

A sketchbook page with studies from nature.

came along and expressed his displeasure at finding me there, walking on some of his crop as I searched for turtles. After that I had to keep to the outer edges, as I did on the more rigorously cultivated bogs at the far end of Big Sandy Pond. I searched the uncranberried backwaters of irrigation ditches and the impoundments used to water the bogs and to flood them for harvest or to prevent the berries from becoming frostbitten in the event of an early freeze. The spotted turtles seemed to be doing well enough, coexisting with the agricultural regimen, even the use of pesticides. But I was not able to investigate much habitat or observe the turtles over time.

Landscape conversion was in the wind. New suburban developments were proliferating, encircling the bogs, stripping away their surrounding habitat, and dividing them from one another. The bogs themselves evidently yielded enough of a cash crop that they were not yet being sold into the hands of developers. If this economy held up over time, perhaps the bogs, unlike the surrounding woodlots and hayfields, might be spared and the turtles huddled within them might be able to hold on. There would be no such court of last resort for the land-dwelling box turtles.

In early spring, soon after my annual reunion with spotted turtles, I set off for the field and woods near where I had found the road-killed box turtle the previous summer. I crisscrossed the bluestem field, looking into thickets of blueberry, blackberry, and goldenrod and stands of sapling white pine and quaking aspen. I walked the edge of the woods, the ecotone where oldfield met second-growth forest. I walked the edge in another sense, too, wondering how much longer this setting, in which I felt certain some box turtles lingered, could last. Concentrating on fringes and mixed thickets, I conjured up pictures from my Long Island expeditions with Gordon and went over in my mind the niches where he typically found box turtles. One has to find *a* turtle before one can find turtles.

I crossed a railroad track that ran east and west; turtles could nest along this corridor, which was so oriented as to receive the full heat of the long day's passage of the summer sun. The rails were too high for box turtles to climb over, and their high-domed carapaces would prevent them from passing under; the rails would effectively divide any existing population into two separate colonies. I searched bracken and brambles, lifted low pine boughs that brushed the tall grasses, then moved into the pine woods. The forest floor was quite open, a great carpet of fallen needles with jumbles of fallen trunks and branches.

Because the ground was so open, I did not expect to find box turtles. But here I found the first one. Settled against a pine long-fallen tree, beneath a modest screen of dead branches, a turtle with a sienna and umber shell rested on pine needles. Forelegs extended full-length in front of her, head held high, her eyes directly upon me, she appeared to be in complete, untroubled repose. She had no doubt been watching me as I stalked all around her. Even in a place of relatively scant cover she could have gone unnoticed, as was her intent. Her head and legs were chestnut brown, her outwardly calm eyes a darker variant of the same color. Somewhat atypically, her carapace bore only a few subtle markings, pale cream flecks glazed with translucent chestnut. I had a new kind of turtle to seek and follow now.

I came to a glade among the pines, an open-canopied place of sedge and grass mounds and stands of cinnamon fern. Small pools and channels still held water in a pine woods already quite dry in early May. There wasn't a breath of wind; all was silent but for a towhee's eruptive calls of "drink-your-tea!" Between the calls I heard the slightest rustle. I held the sound, replaying it in mind, trying to orient myself to its source. Feeling that I was very close to a box turtle, I took a few steps, then let my eyes do the searching. There was not another sound; even the towhee fell silent.

The stillness that had always been a primal method in my looking for turtles was all the more essential with these cryptic land-dwellers. After some minutes during which only my eyes moved, I made him out. From a form he had shaped in the straw-hut skirting of dead blades beneath sprays of new green sedge, a male box turtle regarded me with burning crimson eyes. Now I was all but certain that these turtles truly lived here, at least a relict tribe of them. Because so many are picked up and moved around or are bought in pet stores, then manage to escape or are released, finding a solitary eastern box turtle does not necessarily indicate a resident colony. The discovery of a pair or, better yet, a nesting female or a mix of adults and young ones, adds to the likelihood that turtles are native to a site. The turtle made no move as I approached and got down on my knees for a closer look. His high-domed shell was a rich mahogany, ornamented with bold, broad, abstract letter-E configurations and linear slashes of banana yellow. He was so striking, and yet so hard to descry in his setting. A new training for my eyes began as I started looking for this species.

These eastern box turtles yielded an extra dimension of surprise and delight simply in their ornate patterning, each strikingly different in decoration. Variations on the box turtle theme are even far more complex than the differences in designs on spotted turtles. So many browns and oranges, yellows from pale near-white to radiant cadmium; each high-domed shell bore a unique inscription, as though it carried its own chapter in the history of its kind. Each box turtle's shell pattern was a different way of describing the interplay of sunlight and shadow on and through vegetation and on the floor of field and forest.

Completely unlike the high-speed modes of escape employed by the snakes, birds, and jumping mice I came upon in my searching, the box turtle's escape had nothing to do with movement, let alone swiftness. It was all about absolute stillness. Safety seemed to lie in serenity, survival in not moving. The one action, reserved for that moment of tooth-and-claw close-quarter danger, was the remarkably sudden shutting up within the shell. If I were to put a hand on him, or if a raccoon or fox put paw or mouth on him, the turtle would barricade himself within his own emblazoned bones. The fact that adult box turtles move about, or "lounge," as some turtle scientists put it, in fairly open terrestrial habitat at times, allowed me to be among them in their world in a way that is rarely possible with aquatic turtles. I could sit beside one in my poncho and watch as he ate mushrooms in the rain. Hatchlings and young, on the other hand, are essentially fossorial, and rarely seen. Much of my searching for young and old involved crawling on my hands and knees and keeping as still as a box turtle, as though I were a box turtle.

As that first summer progressed, I went on looking for turtles. I also set up a little studio on a table in our upstairs bedroom, over-looking the lake. I continued to work almost exclusively from imag-ination, but, with an eye to the possibility of doing freelance book illustration, I also did some studies from nature. One was a pen-and-ink drawing of seahorses for the first paper Gordon had ac-cepted for publication. Not long afterward he had a paper accepted by *Herpetologica,* the journal we had subscribed to as adolescents, and later he served as the physiology editor for *Copeia,* the one we had declined.

⁂

I became friends with a good number of my students, and many came to visit us at Big Sandy Pond, though none became a near live-in, as I had been at my art teacher's house. In the drawings and paintings I saw, the poems I read, the faces I looked into every day in the classroom, I found myself in an arena of imagination and coevo-lution, of work and play, individuality, dynamic tension, hope and impossibility, intense pressures, failures and great leaps forward. I witnessed dreams and desperations, youth, beauty, and love, all in an encompassing ambience of creativity.

At the beginning of my third year of teaching, an art supervisor was hired for the district. Early in the year he decided to conduct a master class in oil painting for a select group that I was to choose from one of my Friday morning classes. He had sat in on a number of my classes as an observer and had gone around the room in-structing students here and there. Evidently they didn't spark to him; when I asked for volunteers for his master class, I got none. I begged for some sacrificial lambs.

Several students reluctantly agreed to give it a go, but after the first session were prepared to abandon ship. As the appointed hour for the second master class drew near, a lookout took up his position at the window looking out to the school driveway.

"He's coming!"

Everyone in the room began closing up their paintboxes and putting away their work. Though in complete sympathy, I implored them to stick with this, maybe take turns in the master class. A thriving art class had become a time of dread.

With the coming of the supervisor and the imminent expiration of the three-year grace period during which I could teach without taking education courses and becoming certified, I knew my Cinderella clock at school was nearing midnight. I was also seeing all too familiar signs of change in the natural landscape.

"Laurette, this place is going to be my old town in Connecticut in five or ten years. We've got to get out of here."

She understood. I had found a measure of what I needed in neglected corners of cranberry bogs, pine groves, and a box-turtle woods on the property of another teacher; but I had found nothing like the seemingly boundless first places of my boyhood, where way led on to way. Here there was no farther horizon, no connectedness among landscape elements left alone, only fragments abiding in menaced isolation, relict populations of native turtles cornered in remnant seminative niches about to be overrun by recreating throngs, if not obliterated entirely in the process of what was so commonly accepted as "growth." I could clearly see how vulnerable the turtles were; I felt the vulnerability within myself. I needed to keep to the landscape of glaciated New England, to its wetlands and their turtles and companion animals and plants. I would have to take my family and head north to some less populated area to find a landscape I could be in, one we all could be in.

I submitted a letter of resignation in February of my third year of teaching. The principal tried to persuade me to stay. He told me that at the end of my first year some on the school board were not in favor of renewing my contract, but he had insisted that I was good for the students, good for the school, and he had found support in the decision to keep me on. Apparently I overcame the others' objections; everyone in the administration and many colleagues tried to dissuade me from leaving.

With considerable sadness I told my students I would not be coming back the next year. The seniors would be moving on anyway but it was hard to think of leaving many of the younger students. They were the stars of my days, delights in my life. They wanted me to stay, but they understood why I needed to go.

When I told the art supervisor of my decision, he said, "You are as close to the ideal teacher as I've ever seen. That's why you won't last in public education."

When I left, the Silver Lake Regional Teachers Association presented me with an honor award "for service to education and the teaching profession as a teacher."

The Old Johnson Farm

Laurette and I sat down with a list of high school art openings and a map of the north country. There would have to be swamps and marshes where I could wade and walk without the constant sight of rooflines, the unceasing sounds of dogs and machines, but I would not go so far north as to forsake turtles. Distributions of many turtle species had not yet been precisely delineated, and range maps were misleading; Carr's handbook indicated that spotted turtles were found throughout Vermont and New Hampshire and in the southern half of Maine, which proved in time to be a major overstatement. Because there was a shortage of teachers in northern New England, education courses and teacher certification were not requisites for being hired. I wrote to seven high schools that had advertised art positions. The towns were scattered over the three states in locations that appeared on the map to be far enough removed from interstate highways and larger towns to have fairly wild surroundings. All seven schools invited me to interview.

With Laurette, I set out for the first high school to respond, in the Lakes Region of New Hampshire. Even though there were still deep drifts of snow along the road in April, our spirits rose steadily as we made the long drive north. We passed through miles of unbroken forest and had occasional glimpses of distant mountains as we neared our destination. The terrain was unlike anything I had ever seen; my legs would not be too long for this landscape. When we got to the school we were warmly welcomed, and as I was being shown around the school I felt wanted, even courted. I had good feelings about teaching here, and when I was offered a contract on the spot I accepted it.

Our original good feelings were only enhanced when we found a place to rent, the Old Johnson Farm. Here wilderness and more than paradise enough rolled up to our very doorstep. The old farmhouse had a screened porch all along its eastern side and outbuildings linking it with a big barn, all set on a knoll overlooking hayfields and forest, with a river winding through. The farm property was 140 acres, and beyond it forest extended for miles. The low-level plain to the north terminated in the abrupt rise of the Ossipee Mountains. From the house there was not another dwelling in sight.

Mountains were our neighbors now. A native of coastal New Hampshire, Laurette loved the mountains almost as much as she loved the sea. A lowlander always, I was not drawn to scale their evocative peaks, but I found them compelling presences in the landscape. I liked the way they defined space and gave a new measuring to the sky, different from that of the clouds, my only previous point of reference for space beneath the sun and moon and stars. I was entranced by the way the mountains shouldered against the sky, and was moved by their forms and vastness that seemed so suddenly and silently to loom on the horizon, at once near and distant. They seemed not of the earth I had known.

The night of July first, our first in this new northern refuge, was one of moonless dark, with an enormous vault of summer-sky stars and the endlessly repeated calling of whippoorwills. Their emphatic, rhythmic nocturnes, so suited to the dark of the pines, a darker black against the black of the sky, whipped loudly in our ears even after we went back into the house. On first stepping out into this exhilarating new darkness I had to feel with my bare feet to find the blacktop road that edged our lawn.

We settled in quickly, with our paintings and books. There was even a room for the turtles that still lived with us. I set up an easel in the kitchen, and Laurette had all outdoors as a studio. Sean and Riana had the barn, outbuildings, acres of field, and their bordering pine woods to explore. Every evening Sean would run around the entire perimeter of the hayfield, quite a journey for a six-year-old. We often walked to the small river that delineated the eastern boundary of the property, either down the road to the bridge or across the broad field. In my roamings I found water-lily backwaters with painted turtles, but mostly I took to the woods, the small river, and its backwaters and tributary streams. In the too-brief window of time between moving in and starting school, I discovered wild brook trout, first as shadowy bullets in clear water among stones and sunken logs or darting beneath undercut mossy banks, then as quivering jewels brought to light on hook and line.

I began to learn the nature of smaller northern waters: seeps and springs, rifflings over stone, poolings over sand and gravel, still, black sedgy pools where great blue herons and bitterns descended for fishing and frogging. I followed the footprints of moose and was certain I walked in the shadow of black bear. I also had strong feelings that I was wading the streams of wood turtles. I was learning a new landscape, one whose dimensions I had never experienced before. From the lowlands to the peaks of the Ossipee Mountains, the forest ruled. Lost in their dominance, I began to see trees in a new way, to be among them in a new way.

At school I started my students off by having them make hand-bound books, as I had in Kingston, and many responded as my first students had. When I was interviewed for the school newspaper, one of the students said, "You're different." I always took this kind of remark as a compliment, even when I understood that it was also a warning, however inadvertent.

I'm not sure just when or why things began to go wrong. I began to sense an underlying tension between many students and the administration; members of the faculty often seemed on edge. There was a latent hostility that I had not known at Silver Lake. I returned home every day not just exhausted but with a headache and an incredibly stiff neck.

In the early fall, after school I would drive to a little town beach on Lake Winnipesaukee with my family and dive into the cold water while they enjoyed themselves on the long dock. It was after Labor Day, and the tourists who flocked to the region during the summer had departed, so I had the lake to myself. As I climbed back onto the dock I could see smoke curling from chimneys of camps along the shore and see autumn foliage burning out from the Ossipee Mountains.

Snow came early and deep to these mountains. It started with a storm that brought close to a foot and a half of snow the first week of November, and the snow just kept on coming. By January I could kneel on snowshoes and look down into our living room from drifts more than halfway up the window panes. Snow, trees, and snow-covered mountains were our foreground, middle ground, background. On my short snowshoe walks—I was never much of a rover when the earth and wetlands were covered with snow—I took note of the buds on trees and shrubs. In the essentially monochrome heart of winter I saw in buds a great, if subtle, range of colors and forms, with distinctly differing details and arrangements among species. When I brought home cuttings for further examination, I realized that by studying the winter buds one could identify trees in their leafless state. In the midst of an embattled school year I began teaching myself winter botany.

In a handbound book that Laurette had made for me several

Salix sp.

Acer rubrum

Winter buds:
willow and
red maple.

years before, I did pen-and-ink and watercolor studies from each
tree I identified. Covered with a piece of ancient Chinese brocade,
this book was so special that I had not previously found anything
worthy of its blank pages. On the first page I did a study of a slender
slip of willow that I could not identify more precisely than "*Salix*
sp."; I wanted to start off with a member of a tree family to which I
had a close and deep-rooted connection. For similar reasons I dedicated my second page to a study of red maple, the beloved *Acer*
rubrum of my spotted-turtle and other swamps.

I was learning not only how to identify trees in winter but also
how to paint with watercolors. As an oil painting major at art
school, I had rarely worked in this medium since high school. My
botanical subjects were especially suited for watercolor's crisp edges,
delicate washes of color, and transparent gradations of light and
dark. Subtle yet deeply rich, the colors in each dormant twig and
bud were those of its winter life in winter light. I began to learn the
technique of transparent watercolor, using the light within the

paper to give life to the light on bark and bud scales. With a fine-pointed sable brush I built up glazes of increasing intensity and darkness, keeping them thin and allowing the white paper to show through in order to achieve gradations of light. This process was a complete reversal of oil painting technique, with its building up of opaque whites. The truth-to-nature and linear precision of my little botany studies engendered a new angle of seeing, a new way of using light.

There was art and poetry in this elementary science I pursued, in going out to find branches, seeing them in their places, taking them home to identify and record in watercolors. An exactness was required that pushed my vision and my eye for detail. I went beyond my own eyesight, using a hand lens to examine such minute elements as bud scars and bundle traces, keys to identifying species. The lens allowed me to achieve the level of accuracy I wanted my watercolors to possess. Deeply captivated by specificity, I could take no satisfaction in generality. The work demanded a patience and focus that screened out all other considerations; these had always been central to my seeing, whether in drawing and painting or in looking for turtles. Here I found reciprocity: patience and focus helped me see; looking and seeing helped me find patience and focus.

As an epigraph for the book I chose lines from Thoreau: "Nature will bear the closest inspection. She invites us to lay our eye level with her smallest leaf, and take an insect's view of its plain."

I bound a second book and continued my botanical studies. This was my first extended period of looking closely and rendering faithfully, with a naturalist's eye. I found joy simply in looking so intently at these subjects. It was a path I had begun to take a decade before, but from which I had diverged. Drawing and painting these twigs, so rich for being so spare, and holding the next three seasons within their supremely minimalist structures, gave me a way to celebrate them, to learn and remember them. There was deep pleasure also in getting to know the trees themselves, however incompletely, in their places, to understand something of their ecologies. This art required its science; to the fullest extent possible, I wanted to be botanist as well as artist.

As winter wore on, I noticed that one of my students had been missing from classes for over a week. She and her brother were among my closest student friends, although they were viewed with considerable misgiving by school officials and by many on the faculty. Both were outspoken, not reluctant to criticize, and tended to question authority. The principal, in particular, was all about authority, preferably his own and preferably unquestioned. My friends championed the school's fairly sizable underdog population, students from outlying towns, some of whom lived in tarpaper shacks. They had come, one a junior, one a senior, from a big city—Boston—and were seen as a source of bad influence. All of this came by way of innuendo, as far as I could see. These two were bright and very talented, especially in writing. Our views lined up closely, and I had no trouble supporting them.

One day I found a letter from the girl in my school mailbox. She had become pregnant and would not be coming back to school. She did not want the officials to bring her situation to bear against her, make an example of her, however tacitly. Aware of my deepening struggles with the principal, she encouraged me to go on in the face of adversity, praised my teaching, and said that students needed teachers like me.

She and her brother came to our house for dinner, and she told us she would not be marrying the baby's father. Although she did not want to be a single mother at age seventeen, she was deeply troubled at the prospect of giving her baby up for adoption, not knowing how the child would be raised. As it happened, Laurette and I had already decided that we would have no more than two biological children—we were committed to the idea of zero population growth and wanted to adopt rather than add more people to the world. We had registered with adoption agencies as well as with Families for Interracial Adoption, but because we did not belong to a church, did not own a house, and had a sketchy income, we had not gotten approved to adopt. I told my student that we would be happy to discuss the possibility of adopting her baby if she was interested. The fact that the baby was biracial presented no problem for us.

In mid-March, on the last day a teacher could be notified that the contract would not be renewed, the superintendent of schools came into the art room. I was in the supply room, with the door open, enjoying a cherry cobbler that two of my students had proudly brought down from the Home Ec room for me to try. The superintendent handed me an envelope. As early as November, as our philosophies of teaching and of teacher-student relationships increasingly came into conflict, the principal had said to me, "If you get the feeling I'm riding your back over the next few months, Mr. Carroll, it's because for the next few months I'm going to be riding your back. I will see you out of here."

No reasons for my termination were put in writing, but among the charges expressed verbally at a meeting I had with the principal and superintendent was that I had "aided and abetted the dangerous and degenerate element of the school body." The administrators told me that if I submitted a letter of resignation they would help me get another teaching job, but if I forced them to fire me, they would do all that they could to make sure that I never found another public-school teaching position in the north country. I said that in fact they were firing me and that I had no intention of resigning.

Most of the faculty shunned me. The boys' gym teacher, with whom I had played basketball as part of a faculty team, said, "We agree with you in principle, David, with your way of teaching; we just can't understand your friendship with those students." Another teacher told me, "A lot of us feel the way you do and agree with what you say, but we have families."

My student friend had come to tell us that she would like to have us adopt her baby. She said that if she could not bring up the baby herself she would like to have him or her be raised the way Sean and Riana were growing up. We renewed our commitment but told her to wait until the baby was born before she made a final decision.

After the baby's birth, she found that she could not part with the infant, but then nearly three weeks later, she came to the farm to say she had decided that adoption would be best for her and for the baby. I was away. Laurette took her on a long walk in the fields with Sean and Riana gamboling about. Playing a heartfelt devil's advocate role, Laurette did everything she could to convince the young mother that it would be possible to raise her child herself if that's what she wanted and needed to do. But the girl remained resolute, and soon we went to pick up the baby girl we named Rebecca Anne.

Pumpkin Hill

With seventy-two hours left on our lease on the Old Johnson Farm, I had not yet found a place to rent within driving distance of the small college where I had found a teaching job. I called a friend to ask if we could store our possessions in his barn until we found a place to live.

"Did you call about that house in Warner?" he asked.

"What house?"

David Countway had accompanied me on one of many long, fruitless days of searching within a fifty-mile radius of the college. Having seen what I was up against, he had gone out on his own one day to see what he could find. He drove by a farmhouse that didn't appear to have anyone living in it. He inquired in town, found out the owner's name and telephone number, and gave me the information. But with all that was happening just then, I had no recollection of his doing this. He still had the phone number.

I called, asking if the house might be for rent. It was, Mrs.

Bartlett told me, but a couple were considering it, though they thought it might be too big for them. I explained our situation and asked whether she would feel comfortable in pressing the couple for a decision. She telephoned that evening to say the people had decided the farmhouse was indeed too big for them. Would I like to take a look at it?

"How much is the rent?" I asked.

"Seventy-five dollars a month."

"We'll take it; I'll put a check in the mail tomorrow."

"But you haven't seen the house yet!"

I first saw our new house at midnight as I was carrying furniture into it. It was even bigger than the Old Johnson Farm house, with a string of attached outbuildings and a tremendous barn across the dirt driveway. It stood on a hill, on a dirt road that looped from Pumpkin Hill Road, a narrow, paved country road that wound into the hills. Late the next afternoon I returned with the final load: wife and children and the remainder of our possessions, which still included turtles from the Ark. Carrying three-month-old Rebecca in her arms, Laurette wandered around outside, looking out over field and forest to the near and distant hills. Sean and Riana scrambled from house to barn, yard and garden to fields. We chose our rooms and once again hung paintings and filled bookcases. I set up one of the large front rooms as a place of turtles and plants.

Most uncharacteristically, I went into a profound depression during my first three days in this inspirational setting, eighty miles to the south of my first foothold in New Hampshire. The school year had taken a heavy toll, but it was leaving the Old Johnson Farm that crushed my spirit. Able to see only what I had lost, I was totally blind to what I had found. I could still feel myself in every room of that old farmhouse; vibrant images and scents of house, barn, fields, river, and woods tormented me.

I could not yet feel the warm stones of the wall I sat upon, see the welcoming fields all around me, or look to the wooded hills (one of them, ironically, bearing a sign that read CARROLL STATE FOR-

EST) and the background of the Mink Hills farther to the west. I didn't even want to see the small farm pond or hear its beckoning green frogs. I had no heart to go down to the brook that bordered our sloping pastures or wade the marshy meadow pond just up the road. I wanted no part of falling in love with a landscape again.

⁂

One hundred forty seemed to be the magic number; our new farm had the precise acreage of the old Johnson farm. There was no other house on our hill nor on the neighboring hill. The breadth and wild beauty of this new landscape and the architecture that housed us began to draw me in. Venturing to take walks along the brook, I began to let go of what had been lost and hesitantly turned to embrace what had been gained. Signs on trees declared that the run of Willow Brook below our southern field was reserved for fishing by those under age sixteen, indicating that it was stocked. That meant there would be no wild brook trout there, but they might well be holding out in more remote upstream runs and feeder streams in the brook's watershed. Willow Brook ran on to a river with floodplains that looked to be largely intact. Once again I could set out to follow the water.

On the afternoon of my fifth day in my new surroundings, as I turned homeward after a wade in Willow Brook, I ascended a slope of waist-high grass and scattered shrubs that rose from a small alder floodplain along the stream. Suddenly my ever-scanning eyes fixed on a fragmentary turtle image, part of the serrated rear margin of a wood turtle's shell. My experience with this species was extremely limited, with several findings widely scattered in place and time, but I recognized the pattern at once. I went over to her, fell to my knees, and brushed aside overhanging spills of grass. She had settled into the thick thatch beneath these, creating a form for herself, shaping a shallow depression in which she would probably spend the night. Her shell was barely distinguishable.

My only clue in finding her had been that segment of the back edge of her carapace, a mathematically jagged line separating turtle

Willow Brook in winter.

form from the blur of her cover. I thought of something Leonardo had said about there being no such thing as a line in nature, that an edge is only the perception of one thing ending and another beginning: line is a human abstraction by which we discern shape and define form. This singular line, all but lost among numberless edges, was an abstraction I could interpret. For some time I looked at her in place, storing the search-image of this dream-turtle of my youth.

I pulled her gently from her shelter. Her black head came forth, and I looked into her outwardly patient, wild, dark eyes, lit with fleckings of a broken gold ring and white sparks of daylight.

Laurette made me another book, this one with an exquisite leather binding embellished with gold-leaf tooling. In this I did a succession of landscapes, nearly all of them winter scenes from windows of our house on the hill. Working in series has always been fundamental to my art, an analogue of my deep-rooted habit of spending day after day making the same rounds of turtle places. The cumulative effect is one of observation and revelation, building variations on a theme. I did page after page of buds and flowers of trees and shrubs, as well as wildflowers.

Turtles, trees, wildflowers, landscapes—the outdoor world lay at my very doorstep. But indoors I also continued with nudes and

Woman by the sea.

Women at the edge of the sea.

still lifes and with works from imagination. The wilderness within was the wellspring of my surrealist images of women by the sea and other figures, some realistic, others highly abstracted, and other emblems of this branch of my art: banners, arches, great fish, stones, shells, sky, and clouds. I also went on with my magic-square paintings, primarily abstract compositions in squares and rectangles, sometimes featuring arches and often including elements of collage, pieces derived from my affinity with Klee's work. This part of my work arose from a process quite distinct from my approach to nature studies, figure drawings, and landscapes. The compositions evolved from an inward vision, a construction from imagination that was like a visual chess game, played out intuitively, block by block, in color, value, and line. Frequently I integrated cut or torn paper, writing, and trompe l'oeil elements into these compositions.

During these years on the hill I reconnected powerfully with one of my earliest inspirations. I acquired Thoreau's complete journal, all fourteen volumes published in a two-book set by Dover. I saw even more strength and creativity in Thoreau's writing and the deeper dimension of his observations of the human and natural worlds. I discovered that in his rambles afield he went looking for turtles as well as lofty thoughts and took insightful note of my signal species:

The yellow-spotted tortoise may be seen February 23, as in '57, or not till March 28, as in '55— thirty-three days . . .

April 7, 1853. Many spotted tortoises are basking amid the dry leaves in the sun, along the side of a still, warm ditch cut through the swamp. They make a great rustling a rod ahead, as they make haste through the leaves to tumble into the water . . .

April 9, 1856. In a leafy pool in a low wood toward the river, hear a rustling, and see yellow-spot tortoises dropping off an islet, into the dark, stagnant water, and four or five more lying motionless on the dry leaves of the shore and of islets about. Their spots are not very conspicuous out of the water, and in most danger. The warmth of the day has penetrated into these low, swampy woods on the northwest of the hill and awakened the tortoises from their winter sleep. These are the only kind of tortoise I have seen this year . . . Apparently they love to feel the sun on their shells.

And, ninety-two years and a day before my first turtle:

June 9, 1858. See a yellow spotted turtle digging her hole at 5 P.M., in a pasture near Beck Stow's, some dozen rods off. It is made under one side like the picta's.

An acquaintance who was a forestry researcher was particularly struck with my studies of buds and branches and told me of a U.S. Forest Service scientist who was looking for an illustrator. Dr. Alex L. Shigo was immediately taken with my work and saw me as the artistic means to his scientific ends. He wanted to publish an illustrated book that would be heavy on art, with minimal text, making it accessible to a broader audience than were his papers in scientific journals. He also believed that the artwork would help his research attain a more lasting presence. I was sympathetic to his goals and fascinated by his research and by the opportunity to work with a scientist. Thus Alex and I began a lengthy and intense collaboration in which I immersed myself in his pioneer investigations of the compartmentalization of decay in trees, as well as other aspects of tree pathology and ecology.

Long before I heard the term "treehugger," I had a habit, as I headed out to seek the first spotted turtles coming up from hibernation, of embracing red maples and white pines in celebration. I would run my hands over bark and hold hands with alder, highbush blueberry, silky dogwood, black chokeberry, and their shrubby compatriots while traversing the uncertain terrain of the turtles. Now I welcomed the opportunity to understand trees in a more scientific sense, to add that layer to the kinship I felt with them, the druid going back into the lab. I began to see trees from the inside out and to better comprehend them as living organisms.

Happily, Alex Shigo's scientific focus was not merely on saw logs and other such practical applications (although this aspect certainly had its place) but on the living trees and their place in the web of life. Our association began with the book *A Tree Hurts, Too*, a brief, basic explanation of the process of decay in living trees and "the marvelous ways in which a tree reacts against the agents of wound diseases." These "marvelous ways," and the complex dynamics surrounding them, kept me deeply involved for more than six years.

I examined countless sections of trees, cut lengthwise and

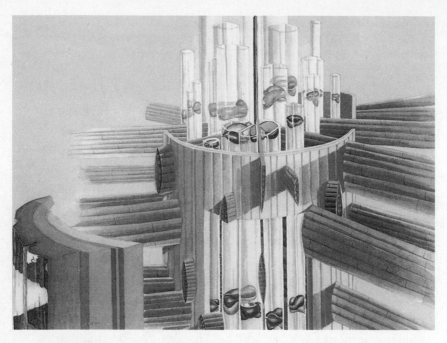

The interior of a red oak trunk.

crosswise; and, using powerful microscopes, I looked into tree cells in which invading microorganisms were at work. From every angle, I examined what could be seen and imagined what could not. While working up the finished pieces at home, I went out time and again to look at trees in the forest, trees living and dead, studying their exteriors, envisioning their interiors. My paintings were a mixture of the naturalistic and the imagined; some studies were as real as a section of trunk of a quaking aspen *(Populus tremuloides)* bearing conks of a decay fungus *(Phellinus tremulae),* some as surreal as cutaway and see-through views of the internal, compartmented structure of a tree, with sheets of ray cells, walls of late wood, and vessels. My powers of observation and invention had never been bent to such a sustained science-based task. Nor had my ability to render realistically and my technical skills at drawing and transparent watercolor ever been so rigorously challenged. These skills sharpened as day after day I looked intently and worked with pencil lines and sharply defined watercolor edges in order to delineate form, layering wash after wash to impart light and color.

I produced twelve large watercolors for a poster titled "Life, Death, and Rebirth of a Tree." Every white—each lenticel on tree bark, every petal of a flower—and the hundreds of lights, as in raindrops on pine needles and aspen leaves, had to be painted around with each succeeding wash as I built up colors and darks. I worked to see and render the light from within, the light passing through, and the light reflecting from the forms I was painting. I tried as much as possible to capture the infinity of lights within lights, darks within darks.

In attempting to reveal the trees' living history, I opened out sections as though they were books and surrounded them with organisms associated with tree wounds and decay, creating compositions reminiscent of decorated borders on illuminated manuscripts. I painted wood cells with invading microorganisms; I painted leaves, bits of bark, transparent trees, whole forests. One of my most intricate series was designed to move the mind's eye into a tree through a mechanical wound. At times when I was out in the forest, trees turned to glass. As I walked along the wood-turtle stream I could look into the heart of a red maple or a yellow birch. In winter twilight I could look at trees, leafless and seemingly lifeless, and see them as being so alive, every cell subdued but metabolizing at winter's pace in an enduring counterpart to the turtles' hibernation.

Several years into my work with Alex Shigo I teamed up with another Forest Service scientist, David Houston, illustrating his long-term study of beech bark disease and other aspects of stress-triggered declines and diebacks of northeastern hardwood species. We also collaborated on a book he conceived to demonstrate fundamental principles of ecology, *The Game of the Environment*. For it I executed a comprehensive series of paintings detailing ecosystems, food chains, energy flows, successions, natural and human-caused

The biogeochemical cycling of calcium.

perturbations, and the relationships between the living world and the abiotic regime.

A watercolor I produced to illustrate the biogeochemical cycling of calcium could have passed for a landscape with wood turtle: autumn rain moving in over distant mountains; swirling sugar maple leaves (whose cells are bound together with calcium); a descending rocky stream with willows, silky dogwood, and cinnamon fern; a Cooper's hawk, hidden sparrows, a wood turtle clambering over a mossy log . . . all the realm of my north country turtle and trout rambles.

When I began my Forest Service work I set up a small studio on the upstairs landing of our Pumpkin Hill house. My workspace consisted of a table with propped-up drawing boards, pencils, ink bottles and pens, watercolors, a large binocular microscope on loan from the research station, a gooseneck lamp, and a chair. When I first sat down in that chair, I never could have foreseen the hours and years I would spend there. As projects overlapped, I began to feel that I was under a genteel sort of house arrest. This work consumed a tremendous amount of my nonteaching time. From my window, looking out at the unmown fields and the tree-lined brook below and at the uninhabited Mink Hills to the west, I watched the seasons come and go. My longed-for hours in search of turtles became sharply diminished.

But I remained intimately linked with the landscape. I would look at my preliminary studies, go back out and look at the familiar settings with which I could never be familiar enough, then come back in to my drawing. I continually moved back and forth between the real and the imagined, the observed and the depicted. By extension, my studio was the forest beyond the fields just outside my door. I went there again and again to look at patterns of branching, shadows cast by trees and shadows cast upon them, individual crowns in the canopy, texture and color of bark. When I went out to visit white and red pine, hemlock, red and white oak, beech, white and yellow birch, white ash, red and sugar maple, I felt I was becoming conversant with trees as individuals, not just as species. As in early adolescence, I alternately brought things in to draw and went out to wander and look, and sometimes sketch.

Wild Cranberries

On a warm, sun-flooded afternoon before frost, early in our third year at Pumpkin Hill, two woman friends drove up in a pickup truck and invited me to go with them to pick wild cranberries. I happily climbed into the back of the truck with a couple of their little children, and we drove some six miles through farmland and forest.

The truck turned onto a logging road, crossed a plank bridge over a broad, shrub swamp–bordered brook, passed between a tall-grass hollow and an alder swamp, then rattled on to a broad cleared area. We parked on a stretch of sandy soil nearly devoid of vegetation, got out, and walked down a moss-and-lichen slope to a lowland fringed with thickets of alder and red-maple saplings. There was no water in the depressions here, but the acidic ground was damp, and the lower hollows, with their crumbles of moss and lichen, were wound with cranberry vines. All were laden with late summer berries burnished by a long season in the sun of their unshaded niche. Despite the paucity of vegetation, an unceasing cadence of crickets filled the air. In the drowsiness-inducing edge-of-autumn sunshine and the lull of insect song, my mind began to wander. I thought back to cranberries and hatchling spotted turtles in places far less remote than this.

Something in the gray-green lichened earth, with its thin-mossed, scant-sedged miniature hummocks and hollows orna-

A young-of-the-year toad.

mented with sundews, spoke to me. I looked minutely at the ground over which so many cranberries trailed; I rubbed some of the clay-like earth through my fingers. Absentmindedly I picked cranberries, with long pauses to examine the dank, warm ground. What was it about this sparse, acidic soil, with its abundance of cranberries and scatterings of stunted sheep laurel? I had the strongest feeling that I was kneeling on turtle ground.

One border of the hollow was richer or wetter, or perhaps both, as reflected by the plusher crowns of haircap moss. Here long twistings of running swamp blackberry mingled with the twining cranberries. The blackberries, or dewberries, themselves, shiny and intensely black, reflected star-bright points of sunlight; cranberries, blushed, streaked, and flecked with crimson and maroon, gave back the sun's light with a diffuse luster. A young-of-the-year toad, not much grown after turning from a tadpole, hopped forth as I fingered among the vines. How far could such a tiny one have traveled so early in his life? Seasonal waters must collect close by in spring and last long enough to provide for the metamorphosis of toads and keep the cranberries going. If there *were* spotted turtles in this part of New Hampshire, they had to live here.

Archie Carr

In the middle of March I went to Florida to visit Gordon Ultsch. After taking his bachelor's degree in biology at the University of Connecticut, he had gone on to graduate school at the University of Florida, where he studied with Archie Carr. My boyhood friend of spotted turtle swamps was now completing his doctoral research in wetland prairies, sloughs, and mangrove swamps around Gainesville.

By nightfall I was far from my native snowdrifts, exploring deeper pools in roadside ditches with Gordon as he used a flashlight to check his live traps for giant salamanders. The next morning we were wading a water hyacinth–covered mangrove swamp, working a two-man dredge to seine for turtles. These Floridian waters teemed with more abundance and variety of life in March than my familiar New England marshes and swamps held in August. Everything was unknown to me, and, as keen as I was to wade into wetlands in my northern range, I would not have entered these southern waters without a native guide. It was impossible to see what lay hidden beneath the thick floating mats and the choking submergent vegetation. On one of our hauls a great brown snake uncoiled from the mass of water plants and slipped away before we could identify it.

As we carefully picked through the heavy plant material that came to the surface in every scoop, we found tiny, neon-bright fish and little mud turtles, even some hatchlings with coral plastrons. I unveiled a spectacularly marked juvenile Florida redbelly turtle, his carapace vivid yellow and orange etched with black, his plastron ruby-red.

That afternoon Gordon took me to the university to meet Archie Carr. We stood in his lab, talking about turtles beside a great tank in which three young green sea turtles swam. They were being rehabilitated from various mishaps with fishing lines and nets. One was an albino and therefore not a good candidate for release into the ocean.

The father of American turtle studies was as approachable and eloquent as his books. I had carried my copy of his *Handbook of Turtles* with me, my Christmas present of eighteen years before. On the long flight south I had reread his introduction and was moved again by its especially compelling final paragraph:

> The Cenozoic came, and with it progressive drought, and the turtles joined the great hegira of swamp and forest animals to steppe and prairie, and watched again as the mammals rose to heights of evolutionary frenzy reminiscent of the dinosaurs in their day, and swept across the grasslands in an endless cavalcade of restless, warm-blooded types. Turtles went with them, as

tortoises now, with high shells and columnar, elephantine feet, but always making as few compromises as possible with the new environment, for by now their architecture and their philosophy had been proved by the eons; and there is no wonder that they just kept on watching as *Eohippus* begat Man o' War and a mob of irresponsible and shifty-eyed little shrews swarmed down out of the trees to chip at stones, and fidget around fires, and build atom bombs.

I presented Carr with a watercolor of a spotted turtle that I had painted with this meeting in mind. He signed my book.

study of a carex sedge. hop sedge   ((carex lupulinum) .)
November. 12 McDevitt—

LATER YEARS

In my heart I will be an explorer naturalist until I die. I do not think
that conception overly romantic or unrealistic. Perhaps the wilder-
nesses of popular imagination no longer exist. Perhaps very soon every
square kilometer of the land will have been traversed by someone on
foot. I know that the Amazon headwaters, New Guinea Highlands, and
Antarctica have become tourist stops. But there is nonetheless real
substance in my fantasy of an endless new world.

—E. O. Wilson, *The Naturalist*

Sibley

A WEEK BEFORE CHRISTMAS during my sixth year at the college, I received a letter from the dean saying that my contract would not be renewed. The college, nearing the final throes of economic demise, had decided to terminate all faculty whose contracts were up for renewal. Late that winter, with deep regrets, the Bartletts came to tell us that our house had been sold. It had been on the market all through our six years there, and from time to time people had come to look the place over. They all had decided that it was too big or would require too much work, and our life on Pumpkin Hill went on. Now that idyll had come to an end. Another convergence, another turning: job and home lost in the same season.

When a friend told us of a house that might be for rent, I called the owner. Miss Wilkins hadn't yet made up her mind about renting, but she said that we should have a talk. Several days later I found myself sitting in the east parlor at Annaslee, the home of Miss Nancy Sibley Elizabeth Wilkins. The house, which had been built by her great-grandfather, was in Lower Village, a settlement of seven old Colonials about two miles from our farmhouse on the hill. Sibley, as Miss Wilkins was known, was eighty-six years old; she had been staying at Annaslee from spring into November every year since she was born, in 1889. The house that might be for rent was situated to the east of Annaslee, a smaller, humbler Colonial that was older than her home, having been built in the late 1700s. Simply seen in passing, Dudley House had always attracted Laurette's attention; white with green shutters, it had cinnabar-red window frames, feathered clapboards, and woodbine trailing along the east porch above a broad door with twelve raised panels. A long outbuilding with two arched openings stood across the dirt driveway.

Sibley had had difficulties with the most recent renter and wasn't sure she wanted to be a landlady again, but she said she would consider the matter. Within a few days she telephoned to say that she would rent the house to us. I thanked her very much and said we'd take it.

"But you haven't been in the house. I must show it to you before you make your decision," she told me.

"The most beautiful door in Warner," she said as she unlocked the twelve-panel door. She ushered us inside. Sibley walked with a cane, but she got along quite well with it, and was still driving. I had always thought that her NSEW license plate referred to the four points of the compass, but I now understood that they were the initials of her full name. The distinctive plates on her vintage Ford warned other drivers in Warner to give her a wide berth. Happily she drove no farther than the mile-away market and post office, except for slow tours along dirt roads in the woods.

Her family's homestead had originally included the oldest house in Warner, which had been moved via oxen across the frozen Warner River to stand across the road from Annaslee. The property also included the Lower Village church, which became hers when the wooden steeple fell onto the west lawn of Annaslee. She subsequently donated the church to the Historical Society. Her land covered that same uncanny number of acres, 140, though the interstate highway had cut through it in the late 1960s, along the intervale through which the Warner River flowed. Sibley had waged a determined battle to have the northbound and southbound lanes divide to pass around her family's ancestral cemetery, defeating the state's plan to relocate it. By way of a deep hollow, through which a lively intermittent stream rushed except during the dry summer months, and a circumspect crossing of the two lanes of northbound I-89, I could gain access to an extensive floodplain.

Dudley House had old plaster walls, exposed in some places and covered with ancient wallpaper in others; hand-planed boards, latches instead of doorknobs, butterfly hinges, wide pine floorboards, two fireplaces, and gunstock corners in the large, south-facing front rooms. Somehow the house had escaped every remodeling and renovation fad of the past two centuries. Out back were fields, woods, and intermittent streams, the river and its floodplain below; in view of this extended landscape we could overlook the smaller state highway that ran in front of the house and the noisy interstate below.

Sibley dropped the keys to Dudley House into my hand. They were heavy, even sculptural, one forged of iron, the other made of brass. *These look like the keys to the sheriff of Nottingham's jail,* I thought as I shifted their weight in my palm and traced their forms with my fingertips. These keys were not for incarcerating, however; they were for unlocking. These were the keys to a continuing turtle connection, to Laurette's and my ability to continue as artists, to our family's survival and essence.

The Digs

Early in June I went back to the hollow where I had picked wild cranberries the previous autumn. Spring green had come back into the reddened vines, and fine sedges emerged from the shallow, silvery standing water at the low end of the moss-lichen slope. I heard killdeer crying from the spare, sandy terrain beyond and spring peepers singing from a marsh not far away. Water did not appear to linger long here, but I was struck by how much the hollow looked like one of the seasonal depressions at Cedar Pastures. Stepping carefully in damp and delicate ground, I walked the alder edge, looking. There is belief in looking. The ground itself was something to see, holding signs I needed to decipher. In looking I felt I was learning; it didn't matter that I had no clear idea what it was I was learning.

A little pickerel frog leaped over moss on which I had seen the toadlet at cranberrying time—another amphibian sentinel, an indicator: *Rana palustris,* frog of the marsh. After inspecting sedgy shallows, I turned to a broad, dry, sandy plateau elevated only eight feet or so above the damp depressions. Beyond it lay a great marsh with shrub-swamp islands. I could not see the whole of the marsh, as it turned a corner in the distance. If turtles were around, they surely nested in this sparsely vegetated earth that was baked by the sun all day long. A small sandpit had been excavated in the slope that dropped to the moss and lichen flats, but it appeared to be inactive. Isolated stands of sweetfern and scattered tufts of little bluestem grass were the only plants I noticed.

Cranberries, toad, frog, barren ground with bluestem and sweetfern—the clues, over some time, led me to the discovery I had been anticipating. As an archaeologist might rejoice in finding a shard, or a paleontologist in digging up a bone, I fell to my knees beside three dark, damp holes in the sandy earth. They had sprays of dirt and eggshell fragments strewn around them—turtle nests that had been unearthed recently by predators. Probably painted turtle nests, they were less than a foot apart from one another. Then, on the rim of the sandpit I found an excavation with the distinctive arch of a snapping turtle's nest chamber. Scattered about on the dug-out sand were the shells of forty-five eggs. I dug deeper into the chamber and found three that had been missed; or perhaps the predator had had his fill of turtle eggs for one night. I filled the nest back in, hoping the predators would not dig it out again. Paw prints in the loose sand suggested that skunks had unearthed this bounty.

I could hardly take a dozen steps without coming upon a dug-up nest. Some were tucked close to clumps of little bluestem or along the margins of a stand of sweetfern; others were on open ground. I found many excavations without eggshells, indicating that the predators had been mistaken in their digging, or perhaps they had swallowed the eggs entire or carried them off. I found many nests that had been abandoned in process of being built. Some were shallow trial nests, others completed chambers. The mother turtle had changed her mind or had been disturbed by predators and left, to come back another time. Almost everywhere I looked I saw some kind of digging. Sighting a small circle of roughed-up sand, I dropped to my knees and became a digger myself. What I suspected to be a turtle nest proved to be nothing. I filled my hole back in and strung a line of pebbles across it so that I wouldn't be fooled by my own digging the next time I came.

As I headed for the marsh I continued to read the ground. It was a great text of turtle digs and even turtle trails in finer sand: scratchings and unearthings by predators (I wondered how many kinds there might be), footprints of deer and moose, tunnels of burrowing wasps, ant mounds, as well as scuffs and scrapes I could not begin to interpret. Intensely fascinated by this legend of the season, I never looked up from its script of days and nights, wishing I knew more than a few letters of its alphabet and could read it entire.

I walked on to the marsh and waded into its grassy shallows, where I sank above my ankles into soft muck among tussock sedges set in sweeps of other sedges, grasses, and rushes. Though it was only ten yards wide or so, this emergent swath brought stronger intimations of spotted turtles. Beyond it lay a bed of pickerelweed, surrounded by a surface-covering mat of watershield and water lily. A vast wetland expanse lay before me, greater than any I had surveyed before. In the distance it disappeared into high wooded hills, pale horizon, sky, and clouds: wetlandscape, landscape, skyscape.

The air glittered with the wings of hundreds of dragonflies and damselflies, infinitely varied in their dazzling colors and patterns. A tiny painted turtle abandoned a soggy basking mat at the surface to hide in the lush, loose sphagnum filling the watery spaces among sedges. Groping quickly, I caught the hidden turtle, which was beginning its first growing season, its plastron still rose-red, as is common in hatchlings of its species.

I felt a gathering sense of elation as I walked out the logging road. All day long I had seen nothing but untroubled landscape, had heard only wind, birds, and frogs. There were no tire tracks, not one footprint in the sandy wheel ruts; only the tracks of deer and coyote and the trail of one wandering turtle.

"Where have you been?" asked Laurette when I got home.

My mind reeled along the day's paths. Images of all the diggings in the nesting fields came to the fore, the many I had seen and those I had made myself.

"I've been to the Digs."

Dudley House

Sibley had never married. She had no children or surviving blood relatives, and we became something of a family to her. She took an immediate and loving interest in our doings, especially in Laurette's and my artwork.

I began to familiarize myself with the area around Dudley House, the open field and deep woods, intermittent streams and seepage ravines, glacial erratics, wildflowered knolls, and vernal pools. Once again we found ourselves immediately surrounded by abundant and varied life. Fields sloped from Annaslee to the river and its floodplain, where I found a new wood turtle colony. On a river walk with Sean, Riana, and Rebecca I caught a fair-sized snapping turtle. Thinking Sibley would like to see it, we brought it to her west parlor, where she sat in the afternoon. She remarked that this was the first time a turtle had come to visit at Annaslee, whose human visitors had included Robert Frost.

I went back to Willow Brook from time to time, though the wood turtles who had become so familiar to us there had begun to disappear during our final seasons in the house on the hill. The habitat was essentially unchanged, but "Kids' Brook," as it was known locally, had more and more youthful anglers pounding its banks every spring, just when the wood turtles came out of hibernation and basked at the edge of the stream. This part of the brook was stocked and was the site of an annual children's fishing derby. Stocking is one of the worst things that can happen to a colony of wood turtles, as it brings people, often in crowds, to their stream-and-streambank habitat. Paths are worn, and the dense riparian cover these turtles rely upon becomes trampled or cleared. In some cases instream and streamside habitat is altered to favor stocked fish, to the detriment of wood turtles. Loss of cover increases the risk of predation and also of collection, as the attractive turtles are carried away to become pets. When wood turtle sites become known, poachers will take them to sell, even though it is illegal to do so in most of their range. The loss of only one or two adults a year can bring about a local extirpation. After failing to find a single wood turtle in successive springs after we moved away, I stopped going back to Willow Brook.

I went to the river, pushed deeper into the hills along wild trout streams, and expanded my rounds of the Digs, although my consuming work for the Forest Service continued to curtail my swamp-walking. As I crushed along on the watercolors, at one point noting in my journal that I was on number 110 out of 120 in one series, it occurred to me that I had seen many examples of tree wounding and compartmentalization of decay in the woods around my house. I told Alex of the living laboratory I had found not far from my door, and we agreed to have a field session there. Upon his arrival he was struck by the beauty of our old house, despite the obvious signs of wanting the attention of carpenters and housepainters; and by its immediate surroundings: the outbuilding with its woodshed, the granite monolith of a gate post, the cedar-slab corncrib up on granite posts.

As we walked through the back field, where I had begun to establish extensive gardens, and entered the woods, Alex exclaimed, "David, you can't live here—you'd have to be a millionaire to live in a place like this!"

"Alex, this is where I live," I replied. "I decided years ago that I would live like a millionaire first, then make the million dollars."

A magnolia flower unfolding.

In November Sibley left for Florida, as was her custom. While she was away from Lower Village I wrote her a steady stream of letters. That first winter she wrote back, "By the way, all your letters give me such a true picture of your life in Dudley House, and you write so charmingly, that I think you should add writing to your accomplishments and illustrate your own work. Think about it."

Spotted Turtles

On June 6, the beginning of the ninety warmest meteorological days of the year in the Northeast, turtle nesting approaches its height. From late May into early July, female turtles are on the move day and night, through water and over land. The full moon during that period is called by the Potawatomi "Turtle Moon."

After my sessions of drawing and painting for the Forest Service, I would go to the Digs from late afternoon into evening to watch painted turtles nest. Warmth radiated from the logging road along which the sun had blazed its daylong trail. Walking this heated path brought vivid recollections of my boyhood treks along the railroad bed. Those were hotter walks, in the burn of the sun from morning on. Simmering heat welled up from the crushed basalt and tarred railroad ties; the landscape wavered in hot air. Shirt open, I'd walk for miles at times, sweat rolling off in the steamy heat and humidity of high summer in coastal southeastern Connecticut. As I walked the logging road I began to feel that I had come home once more.

Painted turtles were lively as they left the marsh to scramble over sun-baked sand. With an alacrity tempered by evolutionary patience, they sought nesting sites, dug their chambers after wetting the sandy earth with water carried in their accessory bladders, deposited their clutches of eggs, and filled and camouflaged their nests. Heated air wafted over me; but as the shadows lengthened, intermittent drifts of surprisingly cool air stirred from the wet lowland alder thickets. Sweet-sad singing from a white-throated sparrow enhanced the mood of ending day. The scent of sweetfern was strong on evening's warm breath. The furtive turtles were utterly silent in their nesting, but the sandy fields and road edges somehow seemed to go quiet with their departure.

I expected more nesting as night came on. The first New Hampshire turtle I had watched lay her eggs was a painted turtle who chose a site along the dirt road through the field behind our house on the hill. She did not finish until 10:30 P.M. But here it appeared that the turtles were under orders to be home before dark, and no more turtles came out to nest.

White pines became black pines against radiant orange gold, then soft-glowing rose-amethyst, and finally deep purple in the west as twilight came on. Mosquitoes thickened as the sky turned almost as black as the ink-painting pines. A potent, if potentially life-shortening, bug spray held them at bay for a while, allowing me to move in stealth or hold still for a time. Spring peepers were thrillingly loud and incessant in my ears, and a whippoorwill began to call from pines gone darker than night.

Walking slowly, trying for silence, I began scanning with my flashlight. On open sand, ten paces from a sweetfern stand I had just searched, was a spotted turtle in the midst of nesting. I had not been mistaken in what I felt, in what I could say I heard—for there *are* voices—as I picked wild cranberries that previous autumn. She was nesting no more than fifty yards from where I had knelt on what I felt certain was spotted-turtle ground.

I stared at her for six long seconds, then came to my senses, shut off the light, and backed away. I closed my eyes against the dark to better envision what I had just seen. I stood in the moonless night with its stars, occasional whippoorwill calls, pulsating spring peeper chorus, and the invisible nesting turtle. Every quarter of an hour or so I stole over to the site, making a quick sweep with a slit of light, the flashlight's face covered with my fingers. At eleven o'clock she was still digging. She had not yet deposited any eggs; she had a long night ahead of her. I dropped a sprig of sweetfern to mark the site and departed. At six the next morning I returned to find that she had completed her nest and left.

⋇

Sibley was aware of our financial struggles during these years of freelance art and illustration and my turtle pursuits, and one morning as we sat in her east parlor she told me that she was lowering our rent. She added that if there was a month when the rent money was not there we should not worry about it; we could catch up when we sold our paintings. Over time her knees worsened, and arthritis forced her to go from a single cane to two and then a walker. She stopped wintering in Florida and spent the cold season at a nursing home in Warner. There she summoned me to a meeting one day; such meetings were rare and different from visits. She told me that she had put terms in her will allowing us to rent Dudley House for an amount that would not exceed the cost of insurance and taxes. We needn't discuss this with anyone else, she said. I thanked her profoundly for her generosity, which was doing so much to make our lives as artists possible.

"I love the work you and Laurette do so much," she responded. "If I couldn't do something like this with the last years of my life, what would my life have been worth?"

After seven years the Forest Service contracts came to a close. One could do worse than be a painter of birches, I had paraphrased Robert Frost in a letter at the outset of this era. The ending of those contracts meant that our economy became even more stringent, but we kept on with our art and I continued to follow the turtles.

I traversed the nesting fields at dusk and dawn, in moonlight and darkest rain. At times the logging roads glowed in the moonlit night like the paths at Cedar Pastures. Startled deer snorted wildly as they raced into dense pine woods or crashed and splashed into alder-swamp thickets. I met foxes and crossed the paths of unseen coyotes. At daybreak I found the tracks of black bear and moose, and on rare occasions encountered the wary track-makers themselves. For months at a time I saw no human footprints but those I had left in a previous passing, and no tracks of wheeled vehicles.

Over the years, expanding outward from a little cranberry hollow and a single nesting turtle, I began to trace a new world of spotted turtles. On one of my June searches at dawn for nesting spotted turtles, I found one in the cranberry hollow, precisely where I had knelt to pick the crimson fruits on that autumn afternoon years before. In a later year I found hatchlings overwintering in the inches-deep, intermittently flooded trough at the hollow's end, a place of sedge and rose pogonia orchids. I followed spotted turtles through marshes and shrub swamps, beaver and muskrat channels, wooded pools, and traveling streams in alder and red maple swamps; into vernal pools, onto nesting grounds, and into dense shrub-swamp hibernacula.

I found a two-acre grassy seasonal pool in which, at the height of their activity, from April into early July, I saw more spotted turtles than I had seen in any single place before—fourteen individuals one day. I followed the main watercourse that ran through their wetland mosaic to sand- and gravel-bottomed reaches where wood turtles and wild brook trout lived. And as an early June twilight was deepening, several years into my new immersion in the seasons of the spotted turtle, my rounds of their nesting grounds brought me to a species I had never known before.

That day I was touring the nesting places with a woman I had first met as a young girl, when her family visited their farm up the road from our house on Pumpkin Hill. Annie Burke was now at work on her Ph.D. thesis at Harvard, conducting research into patterns of development in the chelonian carapace, the evolution of the turtle shell that brought about a unique and complex restructuring of the vertebrate skeleton. I was providing her with some snapping turtle eggs for her research. She was an insightful and dedicated scientist of academe and the lab, but she also needed a connection with turtles in the wild, and at times she joined me on excursions to the Digs. What better thing could there be for a follower of turtles—animals with a deep and remarkably unchanging coevolutionary history with the earth—than to have an evolutionary morphologist to talk with?

As we came to a turn in the dirt road, I saw what appeared to be the biggest painted turtle I had ever seen, twice the size of any other. But I quickly realized that this turtle, with a high-domed, helmet-like black shell and long neck, had to be a Blanding's. The turtle turned to look at me; her bright yellow chin and throat confirmed the identification. I had seen this species only in captivity; it did not occur in my turtle haunts in Connecticut and southeastern Massachusetts, although I had read that it was found in parts of New Hampshire.

Only a few days before, as I waded a reedy backwater and watched the distinct movements in vegetation caused by a submerged turtle I wasn't able to catch sight of, I had felt strongly that

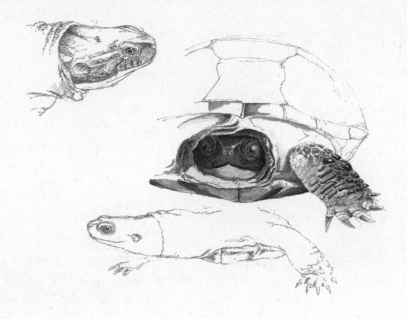

Studies of a Blanding's turtle.

there were Blanding's turtles about me. Now I was looking directly at one, out in the open on land in the evening light. Like the first spotted turtle I had found here, this was a female on her nesting mission. Her plastron rested level on the sand; she had not yet begun to dig. Hoping that our sudden intrusion hadn't disturbed her, we ducked into an alder thicket.

The turtle held still for a long time, then began to head for cover. Certain that she would not make another attempt to lay her eggs that night, I came out of hiding and picked her up. I could see her tracks in the sand, a record of her circuitous wanderings. There were trial scrapes with her front feet here and there and several shallow depressions where she had begun to scoop with her hind feet but had not committed to completing a chamber. I took her home, and in the morning I made drawings and took photographs, documented her in my notebooks, then released her where I had found her.

After that first encounter, Blanding's turtles joined spotted and wood turtles as a central focus of my observations. With this discovery I slipped even more into thinking that the new landscape I was beginning to chart was unbounded. I found myself believing once again that I had come to a space and time of turtles that would not run out on me, a place that I would not outlive.

The Year of the Turtle

At the age of forty-five I began writing and illustrating the book I had first dreamed of in early adolescence during the final seasons of the Old Swamp and the awakening promise of Cedar Pastures, when I created my first handbound book in Bill Miller's art room. The book would tell of the turtles I'd known, starting with the first one. Of course the star would be the spotted turtle. And the star of the starring species would be Ariadne, the brilliantly colored, beautifully marked female I had come to know in the wild over a period of years and was still following.

When I got the book contract, a promise opened up before me like that of the first swamps and streams, of way leading on to way. My original desire had been to create a book that would document and celebrate what I had come to find over my years with turtles in their landscape. It would be a way for me to depict and share the swamps and their seasons. But the years between my first imaginings and the chance to do the book had brought a deep and relentless diminishing of all that I had come to see, and wished to express. The dream had taken on the aura of a nightmare in which I no sooner found what I was searching for than it was taken away. I did not want my book to be an elegy, but I could not overlook what had come to pass. Nor could I pretend that the near future would bring a change for the better. Only the fact that I had found some new horizons enabled me to avoid a crippling despair—and to do the book at all I would have to try to believe that these new places would be spared the fate I had witnessed elsewhere.

I had been aware that getting a contract to do the turtle book would bring about profound changes in my life. I knew I would have to abandon nearly all of what had constituted my own work in art and focus exclusively on drawings and watercolors dedicated to natural history. I had deep misgivings and regret about turning aside talents I believed in and was dedicated to pursuing, about letting go of some of my most cherished ways of seeing, imagining, and working as a visual artist. I also knew, however, that what I would be doing was not just a book or even a series of books: to honor my vow to turtles and swamps, I had to redirect my vision, time, and energy. It had been difficult enough to keep up with my own artwork as I produced the Forest Service illustrations; this new commitment would make it impossible to move back and forth from Cubist collage, surrealist images, figure drawings, and magic squares to natural-history art and writing, scientific research, and fieldwork. I had never diverged from my agreement with Bill Miller's belief that in the end art alone matters in the realm of human experience and endeavor. I saw the need for art and a possible place for my work within that need. But I was walking a disappearing landscape and saw the superseding need to try to help reverse that devastation.

I would have to add more of a field biologist perspective to my fundamental role of "being there." My notebooks would have to include more specific and detailed documentation of individual turtles, with records of their places and patterns over the seasons. I would also have to catch up on the scientific literature and make personal contacts with herpetologists doing fieldwork on the species I was writing about.

Years before, I had resolved to dedicate my first book to Sibley, and when I told her the news about the contract, I revealed the dedication.

The next day, as Laurette was having lunch at Annaslee, Sibley leaned forward and asked, "Don't you think David ought to dedicate his first book to you, Laurette?"

"Oh, no, Sibley. David has had it in his mind for a long time that if he ever did a book he would dedicate it to you."

"Well, then . . . ," she responded, settling back in her chair without further protestation.

At the end of one of my writing days, during a sherry and cheese party we carried to the west parlor at Annaslee, she took a sip and, after a pensive pause, said, "I think it's good, having an author in Lower Village."

As the project progressed, I brought home Ariadne and other turtles for brief drawing sessions. I collected dragonflies, plants, and even sand and gravel for pencil and watercolor studies in my swamp sketchbook, references for illustrations that I worked on while turtles slept beneath the snow. I did pencil-and-watercolor studies of entire turtles and page after page of details: carapace and plastron scutes, heads and feet. I applied the intimacy of my winter bud studies to the scatterings of red-orange set in jet black on the scales of a wood turtle's foreleg, the pale gold striations on the umber carapace, which emerged brightly when the shell was wet (the pattern mimicked that of needles shed by white pine), the mystery in the gold-ringed eye. At my drawing table I viewed as objects of art the turtles, salamanders, and other life forms that I observed in the field as part of the web of life.

At the Old Johnson Farm I had begun a handbound book of details of a frog's back, a trout's side, evolution-wrought patterns seen as abstract designs. Now, all winter long, artist and writer overshadowed naturalist as I developed illustrations and text from sketchbooks and notebooks as well as from memory and imagination.

I also took photographs to use as references for my art. As a teacher I had always advised students not to do this, telling them that photographs contained more misinformation than information and led to drawings and paintings that looked wooden and lifeless, just as though they had been done from photos. But as I worked in the snowbound heart of winter, far removed from the times and places of the turtles, I found the photos I had taken extremely helpful, providing form, color, and ambience as I worked on a pen-and-ink of a nesting snapping turtle or a watercolor of a hatchling spotted turtle emerging from his nest. I came to under-

A swamp notebook page: wood turtle in vines.

stand that after one had drawn from nature for a long enough time, from the actual thing in real light, one could successfully extract information from photographs. Looking at photos helped put me back into the floods of spring or the heat and humidity of high summer, even after a session of shoveling snow and bringing in firewood.

Sibley did not live to see the finished version of the book that was dedicated to her. She died the December before it was published, a little more than a month after her one hundred and first birthday. She had seen color proofs of the cover and art work and samples of the text, including the dedication page, with its "For Sibley" and a pen-and-ink drawing of rattlesnake manna grass, one of my favorite plants of spotted turtle places. We had had fifteen years with this loving and unfailingly supportive friend.

"You do so much for me," she would say when I brought her the simplest bouquet picked from her gardens and ours, always commenting on how much she loved the way I integrated wild grasses from the fields into my flower arrangements.

During my own overwintering I did not feel out of touch with Ariadne. I could picture her lodged in her hibernaculum and envision her emergence at thaw. As I worked, I felt myself wheeling in the orbit of the season's cycles, moving toward thaw and spring. When the longest night of the year marked the turning of that corner, I became aware of each day's incremental advance toward the vernal equinox. This awareness came to me keenly as the low-arcing sun slipped behind the hills to the southwest. I saw it out my windows, in the light carried by clouds that seemed ever riding out of the west at sunset, in the last light ascending skyward in the high crowns of the white pines, in the fading ocher and lingering gray light of dusk on southwest-facing twigs, branches, and trunks of leafless trees.

In my room, at my worktable, like some cloistered monk at his illuminations or sequestered mystic at his meditations, I could see where I was going as I pressed on with my writing and drawing. Out of the corner of my eye, the side of my mind, I saw, as though through an extra window in the white plaster wall, the thaw I was traveling toward: the newly opened water, black and clear, ringed with gray ice, surrounded by blinding snow. As distant as it seemed in winter, I could see clearly the light that melts the world, the light of March's transition to April. And in that light I could see myself looking for the brilliant geometry of jet-black shells in water, the barely discernible specks on the dull, shadowy domes of dry shells hidden in sedge. It all awaited me, and I was being carried there.

When Sibley could no longer manage on her own, with summers at Annaslee and winters at the nursing home, she moved to an extended-care facility. Her room there had the feel of an art gallery, with our paintings on all of her walls. Her greatest joy was to return to Annaslee for a day, but those visits dwindled to one day a week in her last few summers. To get her from our car into her wheelchair, we had to use a sliding board at first and then a lift. It was excruciatingly painful for her at times. She would sift her breath through her teeth but never uttered a complaint.

The final summer of her life was the first in a century that she did not return to Annaslee. As Laurette was having lunch with her in August, Sibley said to her, "I have something I want to tell you. It has been on my mind for some time. How would you and David like to be the owners of Dudley House?"

She went on to say that she had made a change in her will some years before, leaving the house to us. She wanted to have the pleasure of telling us herself.

Tupper Hill

While I was writing and illustrating *Swampwalker's Journal,* the final book in my "wet-sneaker trilogy," I became the visiting naturalist artist at the Norcross Wildlife Foundation's sanctuary, Tupper

Hill. I went there once a month for a three-day stay to document amphibians and reptiles—primarily species listed as rare, threatened, or of special concern in Massachusetts—on the sanctuary's five thousand acres.

Twenty acres of Tupper Hill were open to the public, with nature trails, native wildflower gardens, and a visitor center that housed a museum and offered nature programs. The remainder of the acreage had been left to nature for half a century. Every twenty paces around the perimeter of this domain was a bright yellow sign with clear black letters: "WARNING! PRIVATE LAND Reserved for nature . . . do not enter." Just inside this encompassing ring of signs the healing was palpable. This partitioning, twenty acres for humankind and the balance, almost five thousand, exclusively for wildlife, was a stunning reversal of the way in which so much of the landscape is divided up. At times I was the only human being in all those acres.

The land ranged in elevation from 850 to 1,150 feet, its terrain primarily boulder- and ledge-studded hills dominated by oak-hickory forest with mountain laurel, huckleberry, and lowbush blueberry understory. It was laced with seeps and springs, ephemeral and permanent streams, vernal pools and pockets of larger wetlands: ponds, swamps, marshes, and fens.

My wood-turtle searches convinced me that although they at times roamed sections of the sanctuary during their summer terrestrial phase—I found one nesting there on my first visit—they could not overwinter in the stream reaches within its boundaries. They were therefore not truly sanctuary residents; they were dependent upon unprotected neighboring habitat to maintain their colony. From the road that passed by Tupper Hill, I looked at the largest brook and figured that a stretch of it just downstream from the sign-studded boundary was the reach the turtles were dependent upon.

During my second spring I obtained permission from the owner of that property to look for wood turtles, and in three days I found eleven individuals, male and female, young and old. There

A wood turtle.

was no doubt that this was their critical center, their place of hibernating and mating, the nursery habitat for the juveniles. From here older turtles radiated outward, some traveling into the sanctuary. I told the Norcross president that if the foundation could purchase a "forever wild" easement on the property or, better yet, buy it outright, they would provide a true preserve for wood turtles, as they had done for several other species of concern, including the spotted turtle.

The owner of the farm died the following winter, and in April I received a telephone call from Norcross headquarters in Manhattan. "We bought the farm, David," the president told me. "That mile of the brook you said the wood turtles use and one hundred acres around it are now included in the sanctuary."

I walked the brook on my next visit and found three wood turtles, two adults that I had seen before and a three-year-old new to me. They were secure now, deep within the expanded ring of wooden signs. In playing my part in this, I had kept part of an old promise. As joyous as the occasion was, I felt more relief than elation. Why, I wondered, was such a true setting-aside for nature so rare in the global landscape? This was no human theme park or playground in disguise—no trails, no ecotourism—just a place for wood turtles and an accompanying ecology. It was not a natural resource but a natural landscape. As I looked at the little wood turtle I spoke aloud another of my favorite quotes from Frost: "For once then, something."

At Tupper Hill I found spotted turtles in a landscape different from any I had known them in before. At first I had thought they might not be able to survive winter at this elevation and might not be adapted to such a forested rock-and-rill terrain. But sightings and captures in two different sphagnum-shrub fens and a vernal pool indicated that they were permanent residents, not merely transients.

Perhaps there were parallels here with Cedar Pastures in its heyday, where spotted turtles lived in a mainly terrestrial landscape, with only two permanent ponds, one slender stream, and a scattering of small vernal pools. On my final visit to Tupper Hill I headed to a far corner that I had explored only briefly before. It was the fourth of April in a late-spring year, and I figured that spotted turtles would have only recently come out of hibernation and would not have moved far from where they spent the winter. I began my final search in a broad, level pool set in a slender feeder stream that descended from steep terrain. While calls from an animated northern water thrush high in bud-swelling red maples rang down about me, I waded the pool's margins. One corner, with emergent shrubs and red-maple mounds, looked hopeful, and I pictured in my mind the sunglow shells I hoped to see. In my searches for spotted turtles in new places, my eyes seem determined to will a turtle into being. But I found no sign of them.

I headed up the stream, a steep rocky tumble through wooded swamp. Perhaps somewhere higher up this drainage the land leveled off into a wetland hollow that held water long enough to support spotted turtles. Much-divided water silvered and splayed among black and green-mossed stones. The sun of a warming April morning—it had been only forty degrees when I set out—glowed lustrous gray and bronze on the trunks of red maple and yellow birch. I could hear water rush and water thrush. The streamlets of the broad, braided run disappeared in places, under stones, boulders, and powerful, serpentine twistings of tree root. In the dreamlike haze of early spring sun on stones and trees, mazes of spicebush and winterberry holly, set in a tilted landscape, I saw a telltale light, a dull sheen some thirty yards away. I knew it was a turtle shell. My memory bank held nothing comparable to this, a turtle among the trees at emergence from hibernation, basking on a woodland slope where only thin sheets and narrow trickles of water slipped downhill, much of the time underground. But it had to be a spotted turtle.

The turtle had no way to make an escape, so I took my camera from my backpack and paused to take long-range, then closer slides as I approached. Soon I was near enough to verify that it was a spotted turtle. Moving closer still, I could tell that it was a male, basking on a small mossy log at the edge of a shallow pool I hadn't been able to see from a distance. He went down into the pool, which was hardly four feet square and not deep enough for him to completely submerge in. I took more slides of him through the clear water.

At this point in a cold spring, it didn't seem likely that he was on a spring migration; but what else could account for his being here? While recording his shell pattern in my notebook, I heard a slight rustling at my feet. On a leaf-strewn stone barely a yard from my left foot was a female who had been attempting to go unnoticed by holding still. I documented the male's many-spotted mate-apparent and began to search the surroundings.

I found a watery hollow in boulders gripped by the long, winding roots of a yellow birch, just above the little pool where they had been sunning themselves. I thrust a stick more than three feet into dark water among the stones; no doubt there were side pockets and channels among the boulders and tree roots. The pair must have hibernated here. The water would flow briskly all winter long; the turtles wouldn't have to go very deep to avoid freezing, and they could wedge themselves beyond the reach of predators. Like brook trout, they could abide the cold season in a wooded fountain.

Forty-eight hours later I returned to the site. The male was back on his sunning log, strengthening my conviction that the two had not merely been on a migration. I heard wood frogs chorusing from the shrubby corner of the pool, which I had searched again for turtles, without success. But here was another piece of the puzzle. The wood-frog calls attested to its being a vernal pool. It was only fifty yards downstream from the turtles' presumed underwater winter cave. At tadpole time the pair could easily travel to the pool to feed and breed. In my closing hours at Tupper Hill I had learned that this turtle of coastal plains and inland lowlands was also a ridge-runner, an inhabitant of forested, boulder-studded hills.

For the last time I drove out the dirt road that had become so familiar, got out of my car, swung the long gate bar closed, and locked it. From now on I, too, would be on the outside of that landscape-enclosing ring of warning signs. An enormous ecological

A red-winged blackbird.

world remained sheltered within. I felt a certain sense of loss in personal terms, of trails I could follow no farther; but this was not a landscape lost. It was, and would remain, a sanctuary.

Return of the Native

In the spring of my fifty-seventh year, having stayed away for twenty years, I went back to Cedar Pastures. I could not return with the heart of the youthful turtle-seeking painter-poet, only with the mind of the distanced observer clad in a coat of scientific detachment, a naturalist in quest of basic facts. Were spotted turtles still here at all? If so, could I get any idea of their possible future by looking at the space they had left, the status of their habitat? I did not go looking for love or inspiration, just bits of information. The fact that this was not my turtle place anymore helped me be more detached.

Vestiges of the landscape I once knew remained, enough to take some people's breath away. If I was careful where I looked and how I framed my vision, I could see something of what I had once found here. I was moved more than I thought I would be—more than I wanted to be—by the early April morning I encountered. But the poetry of place was lost in its long-ago translation, a real and dream landscape lost in the conversion to "open space." Perhaps some among the multitudes who came here could let their imaginations, like their dogs, run wild, but they had no idea what had been here. Not knowing, or forgetting, what once was present in a place, we give ourselves too much credit for too little, make far too much of the bits and pieces of landscape that have been "protected."

I walked in along the broad, cindery bike path, veered off to pass through a well-remembered opening in a stone wall still held in the grip of massive vinings of poison ivy, and made my way into dense brush. A cottontail rabbit lippety-lipped into tangles I had to work my way around. Only rabbits, snakes, and small birds could penetrate the gnarled thickets of ancient blueberries. Impossible for deer and me, and challenging to fox even in the old days, these tangles were now all the more impenetrable, having become shot through with ropelike bindings of bittersweet and tortuous welters of multiflora rose. Many areas of the park had been cleared out, but tangles persisted here and there, and in them the last of the most adaptable wildlings held out.

Occasional calls came from spring peepers in the marsh-and-shrub borders of a permanent pool at the park's entrance; some things had managed to keep their places. I twisted and crawled my way to the deepest and largest, and hence most permanent, seasonal pool in the chain. Tall willows still ringed the southern margin, ten narrow trunks with very scaly bark ascending sinuously about thirty feet in the air. At the northern fringe of the pool, several great pussy willows held their richly catkinned crowns nearly as high as the other willow tops. These symbols of spring struck me as emblematic of nature's insistent, abiding confidence.

By what dynamics do living things manage to hold their place and achieve a measure of balance in a prodigiously human-altered landscape? I was perplexed by this toehold of stasis in an arena of profound change. A mere corner in an overrun coastal plain, this pool and its plants, its thicketed borders, its rabbits and small, secretive birds kept on, while day after day the human world raced by.

What of the spotted turtles? I kept a hidden watch for half an hour or so and saw only a couple of caddis fly larvae, several water striders, and a modest assortment of isopods and amphipods moving in the water. I waded the pool's perimeter, then searched its shoreline for turtles who might have left chill waters to take the warming morning sun, but found none. Time becomes confounding with such returnings. The renewing cycles of the seasons in a niche that has been left alone, with a semblance of its natural patterns, curiously arrest the passage of time, at least in terms of the human measuring of years. I felt that I was on a search in a spring past as well as in the present moment.

My next stop in retracing my old circuit was the deeper, boulder-bordered seasonal pool in which I saw my first turtle at Cedar Pastures. Recalling coiled garter snakes and recumbent spotted turtles warming to spring here, I scanned the brindled floor of fallen leaves. Some things stay so clear in the mind: I looked at the exact spot in a little hollow of the low slope of the pool's alder border and saw a spotted turtle of four decades past. In the mesmerizing morning light, time did another dance. The seasonal moment I attended in the steady streaming of the year was manifest. But what year was it? How old was I?

A couple of shouts and the sound of running feet brought me sharply back to the present. In brilliant red shirts with large white numbers, a high school cross-country team ran by. In camouflage, unmoving in alders just off their well-beaten track, I went unnoticed.

I moved through the alders to a pool no more than six feet in diameter. Every bowl of water here was well remembered, and I had seen spotted turtles in each of them. Again I watched and waited. And once again the anticipated became at the same time impossible and inevitable. A female spotted turtle rose up from the deep black leaf pack beneath a spray of fallen branches in clear April water. She had only fourteen spots in all on her carapace scutes, two of which had none. But she displayed full spotted-turtle radiance just the same. Her shell was well chewed about the head and shoulders, but she was intact. If there was a male left anywhere within her encircled habitat, she would become charged with the continuance of her species here.

As I marveled at a turtle yet one more time in my life, people walked their dogs, ran, and bicycled by, so close. Two men about my age exchanged information on investment options as they jogged past. I felt as if I were in a television commercial but did not pick up any secrets that would help me advance in my particular trade.

I penetrated the shrub tangles but was excluded from much of the bog thicket by its quagmire footing; with one false step I would sink impossibly deep. This final abiding exclusion was significant for whatever persistence spotted turtles could achieve in the park. Fortunately, no one thought the tangles here picturesque enough to rate a boardwalk. A tiny wisp of disturbed mud in a channel of water threading among the shrubs caught my eye. I found a foothold, reached into deep muck, groped around, and almost at once pulled out a young spotted turtle. The growth rings on her plastron showed that she was nine years old. Then, searching an extremely tangle-bordered little brook flow, I was again rewarded. Looking landward, anticipating a turtle who had moved out into streamside cover to bask in the sun, I found an adult male doing precisely that.

An adult male and female and a subadult: heartening finds in a disheartening overview. Spotted turtles had a toehold, at least. Many people would conclude from this finding that we can have unending growth and places of mass recreation, with scattered islands of multiuse parks and open spaces (sometimes called "conservation lands," even "sanctuaries" or "preserves")—all this and nature too.

I do not believe it. I know what finding the spotted turtles meant and what it didn't mean. Ecology, or at least conservation, enters the debate, but rarely does it truly carry the day. Ethics, the belief that nature has a right to its own space, existence, and destiny; and aesthetics, the idea that human activity is degrading the patterns and forms of the natural world, making the world uglier by the day, are not allowed to enter into the debate. Nor is the spiritual, the recognition of the right of the natural realm to possess its own nature, and the need for that nature in the completion of the human spirit.

I could only hope Ariadne's surroundings would be spared the fate of this place, but I knew that the unheeding march of landscape conversion was on her heels and mine, relentless and inevitable. In taking flight to the north I had escaped nothing; I had merely bought some time.

The New Land

During our twenty-first year at Dudley House, the forested ten-acre lot abutting our land to the east was put up for sale. A land dealer had already made an offer and was poised to log the entire parcel, then sell it to a developer for conversion to house lots. As abutters, we were given an opportunity to buy the parcel. I told the landowner we were interested in purchasing it and leaving it as it was. This seemed to strike a sympathetic chord with her; her father, a forester, had planted a small stand of red pine on the property forty years before. She gave us some time to come up with the money, but we had just stretched our resources to the limit and beyond in converting half of the outbuilding across the dirt drive from the house into a studio-gallery. And our future income was as uncertain as ever.

As our dilemma became known, though, friends came forth, two with generous personal loans and another with a gift outright, in memory of her son, a friend of ours, who had died young. We managed to get a bank to lend the rest of the money needed to secure the land.

We walked the woods that were now ours. Red and white oak, white pine, hemlock, red and sugar maple, beech, white and yellow birch; painted and red trillium, lady's slipper orchids, gaywings, and may stars on upland knolls; great sweeps of marsh marigolds and marsh blue violets in low drainages. Many of the trees and wildflowers that had been the subjects of my first botany studies grew on the stonewall-bordered, ridged and ravined property. I visited a vernal pool I had taken quick looks into before but, with my fixation on the Digs and other turtle areas, had never fully investigated. Here was a remarkably pristine seasonal pool set along an intermittent stream. It was about 120 yards long, with shrub, red-maple, and hemlock islands and emergent stands of winterberry holly.

Heavy accretions of sphagnum moss mounded the islands and

the deadfall tree trunks in the water. I knew that wood frogs, spring peepers, gray treefrogs, green frogs, and bullfrogs came here in season, as well as spotted salamanders and red-spotted newts. The luxurious moundings of sphagnum suggested that the pool might serve as breeding habitat for four-toed salamanders as well. These tiny woodland salamanders mate in the fall; the females travel to seeps and pools in spring to lay and brood their eggs, with a predilection for wetlands well draped in sphagnum moss. The females, sometimes in communal groups, stay with their eggs until they hatch and the larvae drop into the water. I waded into the shallow pool and carefully lifted clumps of sphagnum that plushed out three to six inches above the water surface, then patted them back in place. My third lifting of thick, wet moss uncovered a female and the egg clutch she was guarding. I went on to find eight more brooding sites before ending my search, as I didn't want to disturb any more salamanders. These were the first four-toed salamanders I had found in New Hampshire, where the species has been very little documented.

Some months later I met the man who had wanted to develop the lot. "You're the turtle man, you're the one who beat me out of that property in Warner," he said good-naturedly. He paused. "There are trees in there that should never be cut."

Two years after that, a neighbor whose property abutted our new land on the east told Laurette that he was selling his house. He had bought an acre out of the lot between us many years before so his daughter could have a field for her horse. He wondered if we'd be interested in buying that acre or trading it for artwork, assuming he could sell his property without having to include it. Eight months later, the day before my birthday in early January, he came to the studio. He had sold his house and had kept the field aside.

"I'd be willing to trade the land for that painting," he said, pointing to a watercolor of a spotted turtle from *The Year of the Turtle*, which I had on exhibit, but not for sale.

I took the watercolor off the wall and handed it to him. We shook hands.

"You'll get the deed along about March."

The Dudley House property and the new land now totaled 15 acres. A thought came to mind: 4,985 acres to go.

Ariadne Nesting

On June 10, at quarter to five in the dim light of a fog-shrouded dawn, on the fiftieth anniversary of my first turtle, I was searching once more for nesting spotted turtles. Over the years I had learned that in my part of New Hampshire spotted turtles often took all night and into the next morning to nest, so I had shifted from evening to daybreak patrols. I headed out every morning from late May until the end of June. Not one to rise before daybreak at any other time of year, I needed no alarm clock during nesting season. Invariably, I awoke between four and four-thirty and was in the nesting fields by five.

During my evening and night searches I had found it almost impossible to see a nesting turtle before she saw me. If disturbed in the early stages of this arduous and perilous process, she would nearly always abandon her task. Then she would have to come forth from wetland cover to try again on another night, adding to the rigors of her labor and the risk of predation. But by daybreak a spotted turtle (the only species native to my area that I had found to nest through the night) would have deposited her eggs and begun to backfill the chamber. At this point in the process she was committed to completing her work of covering the nest and camouflaging it. The ones I found at dawn provided rich documentation: I could record the individual who nested, her nest site, the number of eggs in her clutch, and eventually the number of successful hatchlings who emerged from it (or details of a failed clutch), and the length of time from egg-laying to emergence from the nest.

Through looking for turtles I became an earth-tracker. They are earth-trackers themselves, these water animals; turtles track the earth through all the seasons of their long lives. I am convinced that they begin to map their worlds the minute they leave the nest and that they never forget any place they've been. Nesting season and hatching season were the times when I myself became a tracker. In hours of walking I never took my eyes from the ground.

On this closed-in morning, it was not easy to make out subtler signs, but I couldn't miss the deep, fresh footprints of a white-tailed deer, dark imprints that punctuated the pale, sandy earth and paler gray-green crusts of lichen. Nearly every morning I saw tracks of deer and coyote that had been left in the night, along with the new pawings of skunk, raccoon, coyotes, and others who had been out for turtle eggs. One pattern of deer tracks arrested my eye because it was different from any I had seen before: toed-in cuts close together forming a tight circle. The tracks were sharp and deep, like those left by an alarmed deer or moose running at full stride, but such tracks would have been far apart and in a straight line; this circle suggested a deer leaping and kicking, wildly active within a constrained radius. I couldn't make out any coyote prints or claw marks but wondered if the deer had been encircled by predators and had had to buck her way to an escape. There was neither blood nor hair to indicate a killing or wounding.

Hardly five minutes into my search, I sighted a nesting spotted turtle. She was in an unusually open site on a low rise at the edge of the cranberry hollows, about twenty-five yards away. Her back was to me; I did not often have the opportunity to discover one from such a distance. She didn't see me, so there was no pause in her work. When I stumbled on morning nesters closer by, they would stop and hold still for some time after I retreated to a hiding place, then finally resume their nesting. I backed away into a stand of saplings and focused my binoculars on the turtle. From the fairly steep angle of her shell I could tell that she was still at work in the chamber and had a way to go in her crucial annual labor. It would be a while before she completed filling in and leveling off as she did her final covering and concealing of the nest, so I slipped away to search the cranberry hollows.

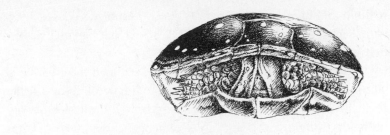

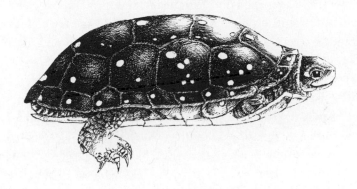

Ariadne.

Some mornings I had found two turtles nesting at once, and one day I found three. I tried to determine from their positions and movements who would finish first, then be there at the exact time of completion and take the turtle in hand to identify and document, then do the same for the next one. The timing could be difficult, as the turtles might be several hundred yards apart.

Reading the earth in the chill, misty hollows, I made a poignant discovery. Placed with strange perfection, side by side on the low-lit, lichened ground, were the forelegs of a fawn, equal in length, from just below the knees to the sharp-pointed toe tips. Alive with color, an almost burning sienna red along the shafts to a sharp white fringe around jet-black hoofs, as though life had not yet left them (no blood, torn hair, or protruding shattered bone to reveal the reality), the forelegs lay in hauntingly untroubled repose. "Altar, supplicant"—words from my deep past, words that had no place out here—passed through my mind.

I couldn't take my eyes away. In time I scanned the area. There was no sign of struggle, not a scuff in the fragile moss-and-lichen turf, and I found no other remains. I returned to the slender legs, infinitely graceful in this final arrangement. I could make an entire spotted fawn out of them, motionless, like the one who never flinched when I came upon him in a thicket and went on to look for wood turtles around his hideaway. I suspected that the fawn's legs, so vibrant in recent death, might be related to the spiraling deer tracks in the sandy nesting field some sixty yards distant; perhaps a doe had circled around her fawn, trying to protect it from coyotes.

After patrolling the remainder of the nesting territory, expanses of sandy field and the sparse shoulders of acres of hayfield, I returned to the nesting turtle. As I approached her, a deer drifted away in the persistent heavy fog; a white tail flag was all I saw. At quarter to six the turtle was still at work. The fog began to burn off, but the world was still wonderfully closed in and still. The thicker encrustations of glowing, pale gray-green lichen had another, more dramatic radiance, enhanced by the morning mist: the milky rose-orange glow of its abundant fruiting bodies. The aptly named pink earth-tongue is one of the first plants—if not *the* first—to become established on bare rock and colonize impoverished earth that has been scarified by natural or human disturbance. The soft but distinct glow of this lichen is one of those ambient seasonal lights that strike me as otherworldly even as they illuminate familiar ground and radiate a sense of place.

Bird calls from wooded slopes and lowland swamp thickets and the steady resonating "twangs" of green frogs from the marsh provided not-so-incidental music for my vigil. The turtle's mist-wet black dome contrasted with the small, moss-greened carpet on which she worked. There were clusters of bluets off to her right, broad areas of bare sand a few feet to her left. With a slow, steady rhythm her shell rose and fell, rose and fell. She, of course, was unaware of how perilously close her site, no doubt chosen with the great deliberation of her species, was to a miserable drag strip through which a variety of off-road vehicles had been coming to roar at frequent intervals in recent years.

As I kept watch I listened, picking out individual songs from the morning's sweet communal medley: rose-breasted grosbeak, yellowthroat, chestnut-sided warbler, chickadee, swamp and song sparrows, distant red-winged blackbirds. The songs, like the flights of the birds, had a way of describing space. Solitary trills from gray treefrogs penetrated the steady, spaced vocalizations of green frogs.

The turtle began to rock with more animation and took up the high-stepping dance with her hind legs that marks the final tamping of the earth over a completed nest. Ever so gradually, the day brightened in a small, widening circle around me; the lights were coming up, slowly, in the remarkable amphitheater where the turtle performed her ancient choreography. Catbird song and mourning dove calls preceded the sun's burning through; the sandy spaces took on a warming glow . . . all these cogs, wheels, tickings of light and life in the day's chronometer—measurings in space and time. Scatterings of bluets brightened as the unhurried sun prepared to make its appearance. Hundreds of mist-silvered double spider webs stood out in sweetfern, low shrubs, and little bluestem grass.

No wind stirred yet. The flowers of yellow hawkweed, or king devil, were still tightly compressed from their closing up of the previous evening: unwavering points of bright yellow on tall, thin, pliant stems. At length the white disk of the sun broke through in a blurred glow above mist-muted pines. The turtle was reaching way out now, stretching her hind legs full-length (I was surprised anew by how far a nesting turtle could reach); she was adding her final touches, drawing in, gathering, and twisting strands of grass, fallen leaves, stems and twigs, and crumbles of earth to conceal her nest site.

She lifted one, then the other hind foot high, even above the rim of her carapace. Her wet feet were orange-brown from her nest matrix. Passing overhead, low in the mist, a crow cawed loudly; the green-frog chorus reached a crescendo; the turtle worked on in silence. From late afternoon yesterday, through twilight and the long night's bridge to today's dawn, expanding into morning, her nesting represented a sustained time of intense activity in a long life dedicated in good measure to abiding. She would not be hurried—or, I should say, she would not cut short her ancient duty to her kind. She was doing everything in her power to assure that life on earth would continue to have its spotted-turtle expression; she was existentially committed to there being *Clemmys guttata* in earth's enormous ecology. She wove, trod, and tamped, then paused to rest. Even at its most exuberant, her work did not produce much movement to catch an unwanted eye.

The fog dissipated. Sunlight advanced upon us as the shadow of the great hill to the east withdrew. As it slipped away from me, I watched wraiths of mist rise up for brief moments along the moving edge of sunlight replacing shadow on the earth, traces of the advancing day and the final vestiges of night—Aurora's footsteps, fleeting, silent.

At nineteen past seven, the turtle turned sideways to me. It appeared that her crucial annual labor had been completed: she was level with the ground now and she had moved a little distance from her nest. She slowly moved away, pausing to twist and scrape with her hind feet here and there, parting gestures intended to confound predators. With just this little movement she all but disappeared against the essentially bare earth. I watched her head for the alders, and as I walked toward her the pattern on her shell, which was now dry and somewhat dusty, began to spell out an identity. Still several strides away, I knew I had read the code correctly. Fifty years to the day after my first turtle, I had been with Ariadne as she nested.

She went off into the alder border on her way back to the great shrub swamp, her winter refuge, which would today serve as a shelter in which to recover from her great turtle-mother work. Turtles have always seemed inexhaustible to me, if not borderline immortal, but the demands of their seasonal cycles must tax them severely at times and take at least a temporary toll. Nesting and hibernation would seem to be the most challenging passages.

It took me a few minutes to find the precise site of her nest, even though it was in open ground and I had marked the immediate area well enough in my mind as I kept watch for more than two hours. She had dug through a thin layer of haircap moss into sandy loam. Tufts of gray goldenrod leaves and taller little bluestem stood here and there around the nest, bordered by trailings of barren strawberry that were barren indeed. As I looked down on her barely discernible final weaving, a design beautifully integrated into the surrounding earth, I saw for the first time just what a work a turtle nest is—an evolutionary work of art. How could I not have seen it this way before? Intricate, varying from species to species, astonishingly architectural, birds' nests are viewed with deserved wonder and awe. But here was a nest set in the earth, fashioned with surprisingly dextrous, four-toed hind feet, reptilian feet. I could see only its covering layer. Beneath that, I knew from many former diggings, was a flask-shaped chamber, its form as discrete as the interior of a pottery vessel, shaped in the ancient shared form of the turtle.

The eggs, typically three or four with spotted turtles but sometimes up to six and rarely eight, are carefully fitted into the chamber, and all the excavated material is packed in around them. The flask is filled to the brim and leveled off, the additional mass of the eggs somehow accounted for in the construction; then the depositional hole, through which the digging and egg-laying are accomplished, whose form is as distinctive and enduring as the chamber's, is plugged. The hole through which the eggs are deposited usually becomes the exit hole for hatchlings leaving successful nests after the 70- to 120-day incubation period. The ground above the nest is then camouflaged in ways that vary among species, individuals, and the nature of the terrain.

I covered the nest with a hardware-cloth screen to prevent predation, not so much to protect the nest of a turtle with whom I had such a long connection or to increase the numbers of spotted turtles in the area but to gather data. The turtles here do not need human help—the population is robust and has links with other outposts of the species; it will persist as long as the habitat in which it flourishes remains intact. Upon leaving the nesting grounds, I mentally closed and locked a gate behind me.

Not deeply familiar with Greek mythology, I had often wondered about the woman whose name I had given to the long-familiar turtle I had just watched nest. When I got home I looked up Ariadne in my old yard-sale dictionary: "Ariadne: Minos's daughter, who gave Theseus a clew of thread to guide him out of the labyrinth."

On my dawn rounds the next day, I looked in on Ariadne's nest. Riders had come by in the evening, and the wheels of an all-terrain vehicle had run over the edge of my protective screen. Although I had had screens take direct hits and still launch hatchlings, this did not bode well. Of course, had the vehicle careened over the same spot the evening before, Ariadne could well have been crushed. Earlier in the nesting season, for the first time here—a spot well removed from any paved road—I had found three turtles run over and killed: two painted turtles out to nest and a young snapping turtle on an overland migration.

Ariadne's nest suffered no further harm, and 108 days after I watched her complete it, on the twenty-fifth of September, I found two hatchlings under its protective screen. They were partially dug into mossy turf two inches from their exit hole, an oval as wide and high as their tiny shells, which they had shaped in their single-file emergence from the chamber. The gray goldenrods that had been only tufts of basal leaves at nesting time were now in bright flower, their shepherd's-crook plumes arching on foot-high stems. When yellow hawkweed blooms, it is nesting time; when gray goldenrod flowers, it is hatching time. I lifted the screen, fingered the newborn turtles out, weighed, measured, and marked them, and set them off on their nest-to-water journeys.

Two days later a second pair of hatchlings appeared under the screen. Ordinarily I would have extracted them and waited to see if any more siblings dug out later, but in a blend of eagerness to know the complete story and apprehension over some human harm coming to the nest in its final stages, I took the screen up entirely. There were no more hatchlings, no eggs that had failed . . . four perfect hatchlings out of four eggs.

Ariadne, a true matriarch of her clan (and I knew others), continued to provide it with young. How old was she? I would never know. The growth rings on her smooth-worn plastron were already unreadable when I first recorded her. From her size and appearance I had estimated, quite conservatively, that she was at least twenty-five. She had to be at least forty-one this nesting season. Was she as old as I? As I measured and marked the little ones—at a carapace length of $1^{1}/_{8}$ inches and weighing about a tenth of an ounce, they were not much bigger than my thumbnail—they tried to tunnel into crevices between my fingers. A dot of fingernail polish on one tiny marginal scute on each shell would remain readable enough to allow me to identify them if I found them again in the next seven years or so.

I set the hatchlings by their nest. Brand new to the world, they held still for a time, then craned their necks, looked around, and bolted off in separate directions. Smaller than many of the autumn crickets around them, they moved like crickets as they scurried for cover, heads down, almost burrowing, keeping to the dark side of moss mounds and tufts of vegetation, black animals trying to be shadows among shadows. Crickets, shiny black, were as reflective as mirrors in the dazzling September sunlight when they flashed by from one dark hiding place to another. The hatchling turtles' dull blue-black shells were toned with a dusty patina from their nest and dotted with rows of spots like flecks of sunlight spearing into shadow. I soon lost sight of them as they moved among little

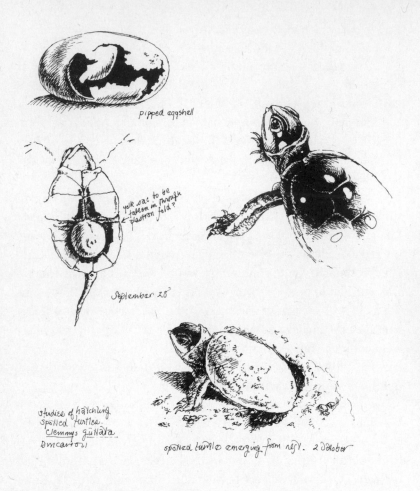

pipped eggshell

yolk sac to be taken in through plastron fold?

September 28

studies of hatchling spotted turtle. Clemmys guttata DMcarton21

spotted turtle emerging from nest. 2 October

Studies of a hatchling spotted turtle.

hollows under grass, sedge, and sun-glinted running swamp black-berry.

Here were lives beginning, not in spring, when so much life is born or rises anew, but in fall, when so much life is winding down: turtles nascent in a season of maturation and setting seed.

Ariadne's hatchlings provided a bridge to another year of the turtle, the beginning that comes even as turtle season is ending. In the lulling light of hatching time, I drifted out of time and season. It was a golden morning in June and I was eight years old. There was nothing before me but the day. There was no end to the watery ditches along the tracks; the Old Swamp and the beckoning marsh went on forever. Cedar Pastures and other, more distant places awaited. I was setting out to walk the shadows fading from the east through the sun of a long day, to the shadows advancing from the west . . . then evening star and one more turtle morning.

Swampwalker's Journal

A WETLANDS YEAR

Winner of the John Burroughs Medal
for Best Natural History Book of the Year

"Magnificent ... the best kind of book ... an admission ticket to a secret corner of the world."
— Bill McKibben

In this "intimate and wise book" (Sue Hubbell), Carroll takes us on a lively, unforgettable yearlong journey, illustrated with his own elegant drawings, through the wetlands and reveals why they are so important to his life and ours — and to all life on earth.

ISBN: 0-618-12737-2

Visit our Web site: www.marinerbooks.com